2

"Jolene Philo is like a trusted friend wl
supplies us with answers. She's done all
resources, exploring websites, recomn
resulting book is both a tool to be used a
Holly Miller, Editor, *The Saturday Evening Post*

"*Different Dream Parenting* is full of practical strategies, tactics, and wisdom to help parents tap into medical professionals, the community, family, friends, and the faith-based community, to not only navigate the world of different dreams, but to embrace it and live life to its fullest according to all God has to offer. This book is not only informative but also inspiring for families. A must-read for any special family."
Jackie Mills Fernald,
Director of Access Ministry,
the disability ministry of
McLean Bible Church in Vienna, VA

"This book is a blessing to families with loved ones experiencing special physical or emotional needs. *Different Dream Parenting* offers sound and practical advice to families during experiences when clear thinking is difficult. Her book is a wonderful gift to families in the midst of crisis."
Stephen Grcevich, MD
President, Board of Directors, Key Ministry

"*Different Dream Parenting* is a critically needed resource for parents facing the unique responsibilities of parenting special needs children. This book overflows with practical information, medical resources, parenting stories, and spiritual wisdom rooted in Jolene's experiences as the mother of a child born with medical challenges. Those who read it will come away equipped, encouraged, and feeling that they've found a friend who, too, envisions God's dreams for their precious child."

)r of *Precious Lord,*
for Caregivers and
Caregiving Journey

"Three cheers for Jolene Philo! *Different Dream Parenting* is chock-full of practical information, balanced advice, and insightful spiritual reflections. This easy-to-read book is a must-have resource for Christian parents who are embarking on the journey of raising a precious child who has special needs."

Stephanie O. Hubach, Special Needs Ministries Director,
Mission to North America, Presbyterian Church in America
Author of *Same Lake, Different Boat:
Coming Alongside People Touched by Disability*

"When parents receive the news that their child has a special need, they are frozen in shock, not knowing which way to turn. Jolene's latest book comes alongside parents when they are in their hour of greatest need. Offering spiritual as well as practical help, this book is a must-have on the shelf of every mom and dad who faces such challenges."

Barb Dittrich, Executive Director,
Snappin' Ministries, www.snappin.org

"Jolene Philo has done an excellent job of researching and compiling a wealth of information in *Different Dream Parenting*, and yet it is presented in an interesting, easy-to-read manner. I recommend this book to anyone involved with children with special needs."

Susan Osborn, author of thirty books

Different

dream

Parenting

A Practical Guide to Raising
a Child with Special Needs

Jolene Philo

DISCOVERY HOUSE
PUBLISHERS®

Different Dream Parenting:
A Practical Guide to Raising a Child with Special Needs
© 2011 by Jolene Philo

Requests for permission to quote from this book should be directed to: Permissions Department, Discovery House Publishers, P.O. Box 3566, Grand Rapids, MI 49501, or contact us by e-mail at permissionsdept@dhp.org

All Scripture quotations, unless otherwise indicated, are from *The Message.* Copyright © 1993, 1994, 1995, 1996, 2000, 2001, 2002. Used by permission of NavPress Publishing Group. All rights reserved.

Scripture quotations marked NASB are from the NEW AMERICAN STANDARD BIBLE, updated edition. Copyright © 1960, 1962, 1963, 1968, 1971, 1972, 1973, 1975, 1977, 1995 by The Lockman Foundation. Used by permission. (www.Lockman.org)

Scripture quotations marked NIV are taken from the Holy Bible, New International Version®, NIV®. Copyright © 1973, 1978, 1984 by Biblica, Inc.™ Used by permission of Zondervan. All rights reserved worldwide. www.zondervan.com

Interior design by Melissa Elenbaas

Library of Congress Cataloging-in-Publication Data

Philo, Jolene.

Different dream parenting : a practical guide to raising a child with special needs / Jolene Philo.

    p. cm.

Includes index.

1. Parents of children with disabilities–Religious life. 2. Child rearing–Religious aspects–Christianity. I. Title.

BV4596.P35P45 2011

248.8'45–dc23   2011028886

ISBN 978-1-57239-467-2

To my father, who lived joyfully
and with dignity in the face of disability,
and to my mother, whose love for Dad
never flagged during thirty-eight years as his caregiver.

Contents

Section Four
Long-Term Care Conditions—
From Trepidation to Triumph

Section Five
Losing a Child—From Loss to Comfort

Section Six
Raising a Survivor—From Fragile to Fearless

Introduction

I Didn't Sign Up for This, God!

Have you ever had one of those dreams where you can't move? The car is racing toward the edge of a cliff and you can't lift your foot to press the brake pedal. An attacker is breaking down the door to your house and you can't raise your arm to dial 911. Your child is about to run in front of a truck and you can't open your mouth to scream.

My bad dream became a reality in 1982. My husband and I stood beside our son's isolette in the neonatal intensive care unit. An IV needle pierced Allen's tiny arm, and angry red scars crisscrossed his chest. One end of his feeding tube hung on a pole beside his IV bag. The other end rose from the soft skin of his tummy. Pain etched his wide forehead and tugged at the corners of his perfect rosebud mouth.

More than anything, I wanted to reach out and take his hurt away. But I was trapped in a bad dream. Immobilized. Inadequate. Helpless. Though God had assigned me to love and care for this beautiful child, I could do nothing to minimize his pain. My thoughts were an inward scream. *This isn't what I signed up to do, God! I don't want to be a helpless onlooker. I want to parent my child. How can I care for him? What can I do?*

As the parent of a child with special needs, you've probably experienced the same sense of helplessness. Whether your child is critically or chronically ill, mentally or physically impaired, developmentally or behaviorally challenged, you want to do something. You want to ease your child's pain, but you don't know how. You want to help your child realize his or her full potential, but you don't know where to begin. You want to ask God about your child's suffering, but you don't want to be condemned for questioning His wisdom. You want to believe God is with you, but you don't know how to find Him.

You're stuck in a bad dream. You can't move. You can't speak. You want someone to shake you awake and tell you everything will be okay. Instead, you wake up and must become the parent you never expected to be. You doubt that you're up to the task. You're worried about your child's future. And you're wondering, *Does anyone understand what I'm experiencing?*

The answer is yes, many parents understand your situation. In the United States,

- 10–15 percent of newborns, or 431,000 annually, spend time in neonatal intensive care according to the March of Dimes.
- 12 percent of children between ages 1 and 17 had medical conditions serious enough to require hospitalization between 2004 and 2006, the most recent years for which statistics are available at the Centers for Disease Control and Prevention.
- 13.6 percent of students between ages 6 and 21 were enrolled in some kind of special needs program according to the National Center for Educational Statistics. That's 706,000 of our country's school-aged children.

12

Lots of kids mean lots of parents, dads and moms who are valuable sources of information and advice. In this book, dozens of them share with you the wisdom they gained while parenting kids with special needs.

Support can also come from the surprising number of professionals who work with families of kids with special needs. These professionals—and the resources they've created—are available at hospitals, medical facilities, government agencies, private organizations, businesses, schools, churches, and more.

This book brings you advice from professionals around the country and provides information about national organizations and resources. It also gives tips about where to start searching for state and local resources. More often than not, your problem won't be a lack of resources, but a lack of awareness of them or inability to access them.

Different Dream Parenting contains six sections: Diagnosis, Hospital Life, Juggling Two Worlds, Long-Term Care Conditions, Losing a Child, and Raising a Survivor. Each section is divided into four chapters. Three chapters address practical issues. The last chapter in each section addresses spiritual concerns.

Parents of kids with special needs often wrestle with prickly spiritual questions. I sure did. Sometimes I still do. So do all the parents interviewed in this book, and most of the professionals, too. Every day, we continue to ask questions about our kids' lives and futures. Gradually, we learn more about how to trust God's timing and wait for His answers.

As you read this book, please ask your faith questions. Read about how parents and professionals learned to ask questions, wait, and listen. Consider the answers they have discerned and their suggestions about how to find comfort and courage in God's Word. When you are ready, try out their ideas about how to pray and use Scripture to hear God's answers to your hard questions. The thirty-day prayer guides in appendix A are designed to help you engage in conversation with Him.

But even with prayer guides and Scripture to guide you, I know how hard it can be to trust the God who is allowing your child to suffer. So I won't condemn you for asking prickly questions. Instead, I'll encourage you, cry with you, and support you when your faith grows weak. When you can't hang on a minute longer, I'll hold you close until your strength and your faith return.

I hope this book helps you break out of your bad dream, wake up, and move forward with joy and confidence. I pray that the stories of parents and professionals in this book will give you hope and strength.

Most of all, I hope you discover the truth God has revealed to me and many other parents. Raising a child with special needs isn't a bad dream. It's just a different dream. And surprisingly, a different dream can be the best dream of all.

Section

1

Diagnosis
From Ambushed to Advocate

1

Unexpected Advocate

When I get really afraid I come to you in trust.

Psalm 56:3

From the very beginning, put everything in God's hand. Crawl right into His lap.

Cindy, mother of adopted son, Peter, who has fetal alcohol syndrome

Eric and Cheryl knew their two-year-old son's speech skills weren't developing as rapidly as his older brother's had. Joel rarely spoke. When spoken to, he didn't seem to process what was said. The public school provided early intervention speech services beginning at age two, but it took five long years before doctors diagnosed the causes of Joel's delays and behaviors.

Diagnoses: Pervasive Developmental Disorder (PDD), Attention Deficit Hyperactive Disorder (ADHD), Auditory Processing Disorder, and Sensory Integration Disorder

Todd and Barb's four-year-old daughter Jenny had always been a healthy, active child. But suddenly, the little girl didn't have any appetite. She grew tired and pale. Her joints hurt. Because they had recently moved to a rural area, Barb took her to a doctor they had never met before. He said Jenny had the flu, arthritis, or leukemia. The doctor dismissed the first two diagnoses based on Jenny's suspicious blood test results. A bone marrow test confirmed the third diagnosis. Jenny had leukemia.

Diagnosis: Stage 3 Acute Lymphocytic Leukemia (ALL)

Alice's adopted daughter Nicole was an emotionally sensitive baby, overly anxious when her mom wasn't around. By age two, Nicole threw frequent, huge tantrums. By age five, she often said she wished she wasn't alive. Alice began to read books and research mental illness. The list of bipolar symptoms matched Nicole's behavior, so Alice searched for a child psychiatrist qualified to diagnose and treat her daughter. Nicole's been seeing her psychiatrist since age eight, and he continues to refine her treatment.

Diagnoses: Bipolar Disorder, Anxiety Disorder, Attention Deficit Hyperactive Disorder (ADHD), Post-traumatic Stress Disorder (PTSD)

Allen was born around midnight in a small town hospital. He was a tad small for a full-term baby, but looked perfect otherwise. Through the night his breathing grew labored. An early morning chest X-ray was inconclusive, so he was transferred to a nearby regional medical center for further tests. The newborn had a birth defect, or congenital anomaly, requiring immediate surgery at a hospital seven hundred miles away. Without it he would die.

Diagnosis: Esophageal Atresia/Tracheoesophageal Fistula (EA/TEF)

From Ambushed to Advocate

Four different kids. Four different sets of symptoms. Four different timelines. Four different diagnoses. But the moms and dads of these kids have one thing in common. Even before the diagnosis was made, as soon as they suspected something wasn't quite right, they began the transformation from ambushed and shocked parents into extraordinary advocates and decision-makers for their children.

Since you're reading this book, more than likely you know or suspect something is amiss in your child's life. You want to fix it, but you also know your child's condition requires more than typical parental first aid. More than a bandage to cover a boo-boo. More than a kiss and a reassuring hug to make it all better. Your child needs you to be an advocate. But, you wonder, what do advocates do?

The answer is simpler than you might think. Advocates speak on behalf of those who lack the ability to speak for themselves. They use their strengths to champion the rights of the powerless. Which sounds a whole lot like what parents typically do for their kids. You're already trying to parent your little one well and make the most of the different dreams that accompany the diagnosis. But as a parent ambushed by a diagnosis, your advocacy duties are out of the ordinary, and your season of advocacy may be longer, more complex, and filled with unexpected challenges. So you are wondering how to go from ambushed to extraordinary advocate.

The answer is simple. Start where you are and move forward one step at a time. After receiving a diagnosis, you should develop a working knowledge of the diagnosed condition. To do that effectively, you have to listen carefully to what the professionals say and ask questions to fill in the gaps and clarify your understanding. This will prepare you to make pressing decisions. You'll also be better equipped to explain the diagnosis to family and close friends. But for now, concentrate on the first things first: developing that basic understanding of your child's condition.

Develop a Basic Understanding

Your child's diagnosis could be a complete shock to you or the confirmation of long-held suspicions. Whatever the case, coming up with good questions in the wake of diagnosis can be hard. Hard, but not impossible.

If a diagnosis doesn't require immediate action, you'll have time to think and pray, research, and consult with others. You can schedule follow-up appointments, or get the doctor's e-mail address or phone number to communicate when you're ready. In the intervening time, prepare a list of questions with your spouse or someone you trust. Be sure to ask about

- Standard treatment and side effects
- Alternative or experimental treatments
- Cure or success rates
- Where to get a second opinion
- Practitioner's familiarity and level of experience with condition
- Insurance considerations
- Locating families or support groups familiar with the condition

If possible, talk to the parents of a child with the same diagnosis and ask them for advice. If no one's available locally, then check the Internet for a parent support group, chat room, or website about your child's condition. The diagnosis information page at the Seattle Children's Hospital website (http://cshcn.org/diagnosis-information) is an excellent resource for researching specific illnesses or conditions. However, your doctor may advise against Internet research. If that's the case, skip the online component until you and the doctor feel you're ready for it. When that time comes, check out the research strategies and resources found in chapter 2.

As your research proceeds, write your questions in a notebook and take it to appointments. When meeting with professionals, listen carefully, reigning in your emotions and fears. Be calm and polite and ask more questions if you don't understand what's being said. Ask for information to be repeated until you understand. And take plenty of notes so you can refer to them later.

In some cases, every minute counts. My husband, Hiram, was taking a shower at a friend's house when the doctor called to relay our son's diagnosis. The doctor asked whether we wanted Allen life-flighted to Denver or Omaha for immediate surgery.

> **How to Make a Quick Decision**
> Pray
> Briefly assess the options
> Choose what seems best
> Trust God

"Can I wait to decide with my husband when he returns?" I asked.

"No, your baby needs to go now, before complications can develop," the doctor said.

I took a deep breath and answered, "Take him to Omaha."

Alice faced a similar dilemma when Nicole picked up a kitchen knife and threatened her mother. "I had to decide," Alice said. "Let them take her to the hospital and have her feel like I abandoned her, or try to deal with her at home?" Hospitalization was the only safe option.

How does a parent make good decisions when there's no time to lose? Over the years, my husband and I have learned to do four things in urgent situations. First, we ask God to guide our thoughts. Second, we assess the options to see if one is obviously better than the others. (For example, Omaha was a better choice than Denver because it was closer to family.) Third, we choose to the best of our ability. Finally, we trust God to honor our decisions made in good faith.

What Do You Tell Your Child?

What you tell your child depends on his or her age, intellectual ability, and maturity. In general, follow these basic guidelines:

- Use concrete language to tell preschoolers what is happening. Be honest, but not overly graphic. Let your child know what will occur in the immediate future.
- Use concrete language to speak to elementary-age children also. Supply basic information and allow your child to ask questions. Answer honestly, but without extraneous details.
- Treat junior and senior high–age children as you would an adult. They should be with you when the diagnosis is made and encouraged to ask the practitioner questions.
- Speak to children with developmental delays in a way that takes their level of functioning into account.

Share the News

Once urgent decisions have been made, it's time to tell others about the diagnosis. What you say to your child depends on his or her age, intellectual ability, and maturity. "What Do You Tell Your Child?" suggests basic guidelines, but you may want to get the advice of a child life specialist before talking to your child. More information about how to locate a child life specialist is found in the resource section at the end of this chapter.

Allow your child to ask questions. Answer those you can. When you don't know the answer or don't know how to phrase it, tell your child you need time to find the answer. In a reasonable amount of time, come back with an answer or admit you couldn't find one.

Whenever possible, break the diagnosis to your spouse, close family, and friends in person. If you have to use the phone, consider how the person will react. If the news is upsetting, call a pastor, friend, or coworker and tell him first. Ask him to be with your loved ones when you call them.

Who you tell is your decision. Depending on age, it could be your child's decision too. If the diagnosis could be misunderstood by others or your child has strong objections to going public, you may choose to tell only a few trusted people. But generally, the more people who know what's happening, the more support you and your child will receive. That support will be crucial in your new role as an advocate for your child with special needs.

Consider Your Next Steps

In the following chapter, we'll continue to talk about how to become a more effective advocate. But for now, take time to reflect on your child's diagnosis. Talk to God about how you're feeling. Use the prayer below if you're at a loss for words. Consider what to do next and who will help you. When you're ready, move on to chapter 2. One step at a time. You can do it.

Dear Creator, this diagnosis is not what I want for my child. I don't know how to be an advocate. I don't know what to do. All I can do is crawl into your lap. Frightened and helpless, I put my trust in you and wait for you to show me what to do next.

Which concerns demand immediate action? Which require thought and further questions? Who can help brainstorm good questions to ask the doctor? Who needs to know about the diagnosis? Who can help break the news to others?

Take Time to Reflect

Resources

- For more information about your child's diagnosis, see "Diagnosis Information" at the Seattle Children's Hospital's Center for Children with Special Needs website: http://cshcn.org/diagnosis-information.
- To locate a child life specialist, contact the closest children's or university hospital to ask for the child life department, or go to your hospital's website to search for "child life specialist."
- To locate parent support groups, type the words "parent support group" and the name of the illness or condition into a search engine like Google, and then follow the links. Another option is to create a Facebook account, if you don't already have one, and search for a page about your child's condition. Often you can post questions for parents and professionals on these pages.

2

Equipped Advocate

John 14:16–17

It's amazing how the meekest parent becomes a
strong advocate.

Janine Petitgout,
Director of Continuity of Care Program,
University of Iowa Children's Hospital

Iva describes her son Dean, born in 1973, as an easy baby.
"He was a good sleeper and grew into a happy child," she says. But
when he entered preschool, his teachers voiced concerns about his
academic progress. Iva and her husband, Frank, agreed to have their
little boy tested.

The doctor shared the results of those tests with Frank and
Iva more than thirty years ago, but her voice still breaks when she

recounts the moment. "The doctor put a box of tissues on his desk, and I thought to myself, 'This is going to be bad.'"

Dean's diagnosis was borderline developmental delay. "Not as bad as it could have been," Iva admits, "but still a life changer. We knew his schooling needs would be different from what we expected."

Iva was right. Dean's needs were significant enough to require a special academic setting and an Individualized Educational Plan (IEP) as mandated by Public Law 94-142 for children with disabilities. (See chapter 14 for more information about federal educational legislation.) The federal law went into effect in 1975.

Dean entered kindergarten three years later, when parent advocacy was in its infancy. No resources were available to equip Frank and Iva for the job. So how did they advocate on his behalf without examples to follow, books to read, or support groups to rely on?

"We tried to be Dean's voice," Iva quietly explains.

Every parent is called to advocate, to be their child's voice. But as was mentioned in chapter 1, when children have special needs, the season of advocacy is often longer, the tasks more numerous and complex than for a typical child. Therefore, parents must equip themselves to become the calm, confident, and informed voice a child with special needs requires.

I was only twenty-five and shaking in my boots when faced with the responsibility of advocating for Allen. Boot shaking is part of an advocate's job description. If you're a little trembly right now, relax and know that you can become an effective advocate, just as Iva and I did. In this chapter we'll walk through several components of the job.

Be an Effective Communicator

When asked how to advocate effectively for kids, several parents and professionals gave the same answer: Be a good communicator. Always remember that knowledge flows two ways. As a parent advocate, you not only ask questions of professionals but also communicate information about your child's behavior, feelings, habits, strengths,

26

and weaknesses to them. Your clear communication will help them fine-tune a diagnosis, prescribe treatment, or seek a new solution.

One simple tool of effective communication was suggested in the previous chapter: a notebook. Sam's mom Nancy has a nursing background. She documented her son's information as she did for her former patients. "I also kept track of behaviors," she says. When it was time for the doctors to insert a shunt, "I recorded head measurements and how his eyes looked."

You can use your notebook for more than documenting facts and observations of interest to doctors and therapists. Use it to journal about your child's personality quirks, likes and dislikes, funny happenings, milestones, and moments that touch your heart. The journal will become a way for professionals to see your child as a whole person, not just a patient. And it will be a keepsake of memories for your family in the years to come.

Prior to appointments and meetings, use your notebook to record questions and topics to address. Preparing a list of pertinent information will ensure that your concerns are raised, and will help you feel confident and organized. The notebook will also be a resource for the future. You'll be surprised at how often you use it, especially when your memory grows fuzzy due to sleep deprivation or the passage of time.

When you talk with professionals, ask if they prefer phone or e-mail communication. Also ask for the best time to call, how often they want to communicate, and what to do in an emergency.

Communicating well also involves maintaining the right attitude. Deborah is the mother of Aria, who is medically fragile and has developmental delays. She considers a positive, team player attitude essential for an equipped advocate. "I slow down to think about what I do and say. I pay attention to how I look. I present myself as Aria's mom, someone serious about her daughter's care, someone who can help her." She also gets to know the professionals as people, so they will take better care of Aria.

Other parents echo Deborah's wisdom. One mom warns parents to avoid becoming confrontational with professionals. When disputes arise, she suggests writing the highlights of the conversation in your notebook. Later, when you're less emotional, go over your notes and write down questions. At the next opportunity—whether that is another meeting, phone call, or e-mail—seek clarification. Repeat back what was said or ask, "Am I understanding what you're saying?"

Another parent says, "You must be calm and respectful. You have every reason to be as kind as possible. There's no reason to be nasty, and it's not helpful to scream at anyone. You won't get them on your side, even if they're wrong." Then she adds an interesting perspective: "You're there first to advocate for your child, but it doesn't hurt to educate. What you teach them may help another child."

Be an Effective Researcher

Another way for parents to become equipped advocates is through research. The need for and amount of research will vary, depending on the child's circumstances.

Some conditions have a standard course of treatment with a record of documented success. In those cases, parents may need to ask only a few questions before agreeing to move forward.

Other conditions require the attention of specialists and sometimes involve new or improved treatments, breakthroughs, or experimental procedures. In those cases, research can make parents better advocates and decision makers.

A second opinion is often the way to start your research. Ask the practitioner who made the diagnosis for a referral. Check with other parents about who treated their child. Often national, regional, or state organizations specific to your child's condition have lists of specialists in a particular field, so contact them also. Be sure to check with your insurance company before making appointments or moving forward.

Three Questions to Ask Professionals

Shannon's son struggles with elusive joint pain and digestive issues. She developed three questions to elicit answers from professionals:

- What are the pros and cons of the course of treatment you're suggesting?
- What can we expect as treatment moves forward?
- If this doesn't work, what's the next step?

The final question allows Shannon to stay calm in the face of an uncertain future.

When seeking a practitioner for a second opinion, and perhaps a specialist, look beyond his or her technical competency. You should look for someone who talks directly to your child and recognizes the living, breathing person beyond the diagnosis. One mom advises, "Look for someone who's a team player, someone who works for you." She says the best places to locate professionals with those qualities are parent networks. "And trust your mommy hunch," she adds.

Profitable research requires a clear purpose. Without one, your efforts will be unproductive. As you begin your research, define the purpose for conducting it. If your purpose is to confirm the soundness of a suggested treatment, look for leaders in the field: hospitals where treatments originated, doctors who conducted the research, educators with proven methods, mental health professionals with documented results. If your purpose is to locate parents and kids with similar experiences, look for national organizations specific to your family's concerns and parent support groups. If your purpose is to gather information about experimental treatments, seek out pioneering organizations and professionals who conduct legitimate field tests.

Once your purpose is clear, you can tap into the wealth of resources readily available on the Internet. Here are a few ways to start your search.

- Visit health information website pages at major research hospitals: Mayo Clinic, Johns Hopkins, and Cleveland Clinic.
- Check out the online medical library at Phoenix Children's Hospital.
- Go to websites devoted the special needs of children: March of Dimes and Easter Seals.
- Find a national or international organization dedicated to specific pediatric illnesses or conditions such as United Cerebral Palsy, the Autism Society of America, the Hydrocephalus Foundation, and the Juvenile Diabetes Research Foundation International.
- Join online parent support groups, especially if your child's condition is very rare. Such groups allow parents to maintain anonymity.

Links to these and other resources can be found at the end of this chapter.

The Internet is a boon for research, but parents should also take advantage of these traditional resources.

- Visit the parents' library at the children's hospital nearest you.
- Ask the practitioners working with your child for a book list, copies of research papers, and other information pertinent to your child's condition.
- Attend parent workshops and conferences sponsored by hospitals, schools, and special needs support organizations.
- Seek the opinions of experienced nurses or teachers.
- Attend a support group in person.

Research Dos and Don'ts

Do   Use the Internet to find organizations that specialize in your child's diagnosed condition.

       Seek reliable resources beyond the Internet.

       Put your faith in the God who created your child and knows the days ordained for your child.

Don't Use the Internet to diagnose a child's condition.

       Research if a professional you respect advises against it. They may realize that you're too vulnerable to handle what you'll read there.

       Put faith only in your efforts.

As your research progresses, remember that at some point it must end and a decision must be made. When that time comes, pray for wisdom. Then make the best decision you can and move forward with confidence.

Be an Effective Organizer

To be an effective advocate, your research findings and other paperwork must be easily accessible. Thanks to the notebook where you write questions and log pertinent information, you've already started an organizational system. Now add a three-ring binder or file folders to keep track of paperwork you'll receive. On your computer, create clearly labeled electronic folders and Internet bookmarks for documents and websites, and you're in business.

If your child's diagnosis doesn't require hospitalization, use your notebook for more than writing down questions and logging information. Use it to record observations about how your child responds to therapies and treatments. Track behavior patterns at home, school, and social events. Document new skills learned, new vocabulary acquired, or situations that lead to regressive behavior. Your observations, consistently and carefully recorded, will be a powerful tool in your role as an advocate. They can be a valuable resource for medical and educational professionals as they evaluate the effectiveness of present treatments and consider the need for new interventions.

If your child's treatment includes hospitalization, ask a social worker, child life specialist, or family-centered care representative if they provide a care notebook (see page 67). If they don't, you can make your own by downloading forms created by Terri Mauro at About.com (http://specialchildren.about.com/od/medicalissues/qt /notebook.htm) or the Seattle Children's Hospital (http://cshcn.org /planning-record-keeping/care-notebook).

The book *One Step at a Time* was created to aid parents who want to keep a record of their child's hospital stay. Written by Jennifer Smith, a PICU nurse, and Bradie Kvinsland, a child life specialist, this book has pages for recording medical information, journaling, and adding pictures. You can order *One Step at a Time* at Amazon.com.

John and Tiffany use everyday technology to document their daughter's frequent hospitalizations due to a rare bleeding disorder. Tiffany says, "When Annika's in the hospital, I record everything on my laptop if I had time to grab it before we left. Otherwise, I send an e-mail to my computer from my iPhone. At home, I record every-thing on a large dry-erase board. At the end of the month, I take a picture of it with my phone and send that to the computer." She con-tinues, "Since Annika gets the same drugs as hemophilia patients, we keep track of when to order medicine and supplies with a new smart phone app developed for them."

Chuck and Lainie's son Christian was born prematurely. Because of breathing issues, he was hospitalized frequently during his first four years of life. Lainie created her own documentation chart on her computer, modeling it after those used in the hospital. The similar format made record keeping easier. See appendix C for the chart.

Be a Parent First

When my children were young, I tended to put tasks ahead of people. But I knew my priorities were sending the wrong message to my family. So I began praying the same thing every morning: *God, teach me to put people ahead of tasks and to trust your agenda over mine.* Gradually, God answered that prayer. He showed me how to put people first more often and let me see that if I concentrated on people first, somehow the essential tasks got done too.

As you become your child's voice, remember that balance is an essential component of effective advocacy. You'll be a better advocate if your day blends research and organizational tasks with family time.

Try asking God to bring balance to your new, crazy life. Then be prepared for Him to answer in creative and surprising ways. Be prepared to become the advocate He created you to be.

Dear Jesus, are you sure you know what you are doing by expecting me to advocate for my child? I don't feel prepared. I don't know where to start. Yet I know you asked the Father to send His Spirit of Truth as my Friend and Advocate. Make me sensitive to the Spirit's constant presence. By His example, teach me to advocate on behalf of my child.

How can I improve my communication skills and attitude to become a stronger voice for my child? What research needs to be done? How will I organize information? Is a second opinion necessary?

Take Time to Reflect

Resources
General Information

- *Exceptional Parent* magazine: www.eparent.com
- *Parenting Special Needs* online magazine: www.parentingspecialneeds.org
- How to get a second opinion: www.womenshealth.gov/tools/secondopinion.cfm.

Hospital Resources

- Cleveland Clinic: http://my.clevelandclinic.org/childrens-hospital/default.aspx
- Mayo Clinic Children's Hospital: www.mayoclinic.org/childrenshospital
- Phoenix Children's Hospital's Emily Center: www.phoenixchildrens.com/health-information
- St. Jude's Research Hospital: www.stjude.org
- The National Association of Children's Hospitals and Related Institutions (NACHRI): www.childrenshospitals.net. NACHRI maintains a directory of children's hospitals in the United States, Canada, and Australia. Click on the "hospital directory" link to search by state, country, board-certified specialties, care delivery programs, current research, or keywords.

General Special Needs Websites

- Easter Seals: www.easterseals.com
- March of Dimes: www.marchofdimes.com

Specific Special Needs Websites

- Autism Society of America: www.autism-society.org
- Hydrocephalus Foundation: www.hydrocephalus.org
- United Cerebral Palsy: www.ucp.org
- Juvenile Diabetes Research Foundation International: www.jdrf.org

Organizational Resources

- Seattle's Children's Hospital provides parent care notebook forms and care plans for teens learning to manage their own care at http://cshcn.org.
- Teri Mauro provides instructions on how to create a care notebook at http://specialchildren.about.com/od/medicalissues/qt /notebook.htm. Scroll down to the middle of the page and click on the link "Care Notebook."
- Jennifer Smith and Bradie Kvinsland's book, *One Step at a Time,* can be ordered at Amazon.com and other booksellers.
- Lainie's chart is reproduced in appendix C and available for download at www.differentdream.com/2011/02/a-trait-to -cultivate-documentation.

3

Resourceful Advocate

You can be sure that God will take care of everything you need, his generosity exceeding even
yours in the glory that pours from Jesus.

Philippians 4:19

Don't be afraid to ask for things, even phone chargers and computer cords. Tell us about your problems and concerns.

Janelle Holst Kamba, Pediatric Social Worker,
Blank Children's Hospital

The moment the doctor diagnosed our newborn son's condition and described the surgery required to save his life, a torrent
of questions flooded my brain. Most of them were what I thought a
concerned, loving parent should ask. Will he live? Will the separation from us traumatize him? How much pain will he have? Will he
remember it?

Some of the questions were practical. What if our insurance doesn't cover the bills? How will we pay for gas for the long trip? How will we pay for meals? Where will we stay when we arrive? How will we keep friends and family updated?

To be honest, my preoccupation with logistical questions shocked me. My baby was fighting for his life and being flown to a hospital 750 miles away for surgery, and I was worrying about insurance and logistics. What kind of parent was I?

Why wasn't I wringing my hands, ridden with angst? Why wasn't I being holy, praying and reading the Bible? Why wasn't I crying? Surely crying would have been a better demonstration of love than sitting there dry-eyed and numb, trying to remember if the checking account had enough money in it to pay for a cross-country trip.

Racked with guilt, alone in the hospital while my husband drove ninety miles home to pack our suitcases, I felt completely useless. I couldn't hold our baby. I couldn't help my husband. I couldn't do a thing.

Then again, maybe I could.

In 1982, hospital rooms didn't have phones, and the nearest things to cell phones were gadgets in James Bond movies. So I reached for the call button and asked a nurse to wheel me to the nurses' station. Then I dialed the business manager at my workplace and asked about our insurance coverage.

Was our son covered even though he'd been born before he officially went on our policy?

Yes.

Did the policy pay for treatment in another state?

Yes.

Did we need to sign anything before we left to join our son?

No.

With each answer, my guilt eased and my confidence grew. My questions were necessary. The answers provided information for our upcoming journey. By asking them, I learned another lesson. I wasn't helpless. I was a resourceful parent, and gathering information was a way to advocate for our son.

It's a way for you to advocate also. Whether your child's condition requires emergency medical treatment, a second opinion, early childhood intervention, changes in the school setting, behavioral therapy, or mental health consultations, you have logistical concerns. This chapter will help you clarify those concerns and gather resources to ease them.

Resourceful Parents Ask about Insurance

When it comes to practical concerns, resourceful parents begin by asking the *right questions*. Not only do they ask the right questions, they ask the *right people* the right questions. Furthermore, they ask the right people the right questions in the *right order*. In most cases, the right order starts with the insurance company, so let's begin there.

You should contact your insurance company as soon as possible after diagnosis. Before you call, write down questions in your new constant companion, that handy-dandy notebook that keeps getting mentioned. Log the date and time of all calls. Write down the name of the person who takes the call, along with an extension number.

Once you document those details, explain your child's diagnosis and situation. Ask questions about your coverage, including stipulations about hospitals and doctors in the company's network, policies concerning second opinions, and/or coverage for mental health diagnoses. Write down the answers and repeat them to the person to be sure you understand one another. If you aren't satisfied with what you're told, ask to speak to a manager. Then repeat the whole process, logging numbers, extensions, and names. If you aren't satisfied, end the call and ask the hospital social worker for assistance.

Resourceful Parents Tap into What's Available

A huge network of resources has been created for families of kids with special needs. Your biggest problem won't be lack of assistance

Tips for Dealing with Insurance Companies

- Log every call to insurance companies in a notebook. Record the time and date, the name and extension of the person who assisted you, and your questions and their answers.
- Ask a hospital social worker for assistance. They are experienced at dealing with insurance companies. Even if your insurance company is cooperative, let the social worker deal with insurance matters so you can concentrate on your child.
- Enlist the support of business office personnel if your child is treated in a clinic setting. They deal with insurance companies every day and will pursue payment. After all, they have a vested interest in collecting the money due them.
- Contact your state's insurance department for advice about how to proceed or to file a complaint, if necessary. An Internet search with the name of your state followed by the words "state department of insurance" should yield the necessary contact information.

but finding what's available. If your child is being treated at a children's hospital, more than likely the nurses caring for your child or a social worker will provide information about lodging, meal vouchers, laundry facilities, cell phone chargers, and maybe even travel assistance. But if they don't, ask, ask, ask.

If no one can answer your questions, you may have to investigate on your own. The following resources are good places to start.

Shriners' Hospitals for Children. Depending on the diagnosis, a Shriners' Hospital for Children may be a treatment option for your child. A network of twenty-two hospitals in the Unites States provides care for children (through age eighteen) with orthopedic conditions, burns, spinal cord injuries, and cleft lip and palate. Children are treated regardless of ability to pay.

Lodging. Several inexpensive lodging options are available for families of kids undergoing inpatient or outpatient treatment at major children's hospitals. Ronald McDonald Houses are the most well known. Other organizations like the National Association of Hospital Hospitality Houses and the Believe in Tomorrow Children's Foundation provide similar services, though they may be limited to certain regions of the country or to specific health conditions like cancer or heart disease.

Most hospitals allow at least one parent to sleep in a child's room, though that is not always the case in intensive care. If your child is in neonatal or pediatric intensive care, ask what arrangements the hospital makes for parents. If nothing is available, ask about emergency vouchers for area hotels or for a list of hotels offering medical discounts.

Another option is to tap into your network of family and friends. Someone near the hospital may be willing to house you. Accept the offer and enjoy a little time away from the hospital when you can.

Meals. Generally parents receive little assistance in this area. At best, the hospital offers cafeteria meal discounts for parents. Sometimes the hospital provides refrigerators in patients' rooms or a nourishment room where families can prepare a meal. Families staying at a Ronald McDonald House can use kitchen facilities and the food provided. Often service organizations cook supper for families at their local Ronald McDonald House, so ask the office staff about upcoming events.

If paying for meals is a financial hardship, tell someone—a social worker, chaplain, pastor, coworkers, family, or friends. Hospital staff may be aware of programs that grant meal vouchers for situations like yours.

Financial Assistance beyond Insurance

The more complex your child's needs are, the more financial assistance is available. The suggestions below are listed from greatest to least complexity:

- If your child is a preemie, a newborn in neonatal intensive care (NICU), or a medically fragile child who will have significant needs after discharge from the hospital, a hospital social worker should acquaint you with medical assistance available through state and federal government programs. More detailed descriptions of these programs can be found in chapter 13. Social workers will also help with applications, which are not user friendly. If no one has talked to you yet, contact a social worker or the continuity of care department at once.

- If your child doesn't require hospitalization but needs significant physical care or has mental health issues, a diagnosis on the autism spectrum, or developmental delays, your pediatrician should connect you with a social worker. If that doesn't happen, contact your nearest children's hospital to talk to a social worker or call the Department of Human Services (DHS) and start asking questions.

- If your child will recover fully from hospitalization but you can't pay the bill, visit the financial aid office—unless they've already visited you—and set your mind at ease. Often hospitals, especially nonprofit or teaching ones, offer financial assistance that reduces or waives fees. Documentation about income may be required to determine your eligibility.

- If your child receives treatment through a clinic, talk to someone in the business office about payment options. Most will work with you to set up a payment plan, even if you pay only twenty dollars a month. Business offices welcome consistent, small payments and consider them good faith efforts.

Your family, friends, and church members will be eager to help, so swallow your pride and tell the truth. When they ask what they can do, request gift cards to restaurants near the hospital or suggest they bring a picnic to the hospital and eat with you. You could even ask a friend to coordinate the restaurant gift card giving or meal delivery efforts to avoid duplication and confusion. More information on that topic can be found on page 128 in chapter 11.

Travel Assistance. Travel costs to and from appointments, treatments, or hospitals accumulate quickly. Again, the social worker may be able to connect you to organizations that offer free or reduced airline travel or gas cards. The websites of several travel assistance organizations are listed in the resource section of this chapter. Some airlines also offer assistance, so call them to explain your situation.

Financial Assistance Programs. Even if your insurance company is cooperative and your coverage is stellar, the deductibles and co-pays for hospital stays, clinic appointments, and treatment sessions can strain budgets.

Often parents worry unnecessarily about how to cover these expenses. They don't realize that financial assistance programs, both private and governmental, exist for families of children with special needs. Your family may qualify for some of them, depending on your child's diagnosis. See "Financial Assistance beyond Insurance" to learn how to tap into available funds.

Philanthropic Organizations. State and national organizations specific to your child's condition may offer financial assistance for treatment-related lodging, travel, and meals. Check with the United Way, March of Dimes, Easter Seals, or Variety Clubs. Local service organizations like the Elks, Rotary, Kiwanas, and Jaycees often provide or raise funds. And certainly, inform your church. It may have a special fund for families with unexpected financial needs.

Resourceful Parents Stop to Pray

Are you having trouble processing all these suggestions? Is your brain on information overload? Are you panicking a little, trying to decide what to do next? Stop for a moment, take a deep breath, and pray. Ask God to show you one practical matter—that's right, just one—to pursue immediately.

If something came to mind, decide how to deal with it. When that matter is resolved, ask God to show you a new one. Then another, and another. God created us as linear human beings, designed to do one thing at a time. That's how He wants resourceful parents to operate. One breath at a time. One prayer at a time. One challenge at a time.

Dear Provider, I'm reeling from the implications of this diagnosis. I want to concentrate on my child, but worries about the unknown future keep intruding. Help me to rest in your promise to provide everything we need. Help me trust you to reveal the resources we need, one at a time.

When has God provided for my needs in the past? How will those memories help me trust His provision today? What are the immediate needs? What next step does God want me to take?

Take Time to Reflect

Resources

General Assistance

- Easter Seals: www.easterseals.com
- March of Dimes: www.marchofdimes.com
- Shriners' Children's Hospitals: www.shrinershq.org, 800-237-5055
- United Way: www.liveunited.org
- Variety Clubs: www.usvariety.org

Lodging Assistance

- Ronald McDonald Houses: www.rmhc.org, 630-623-7048
- National Association of Hospital Hospitality Houses: www.nahhh.org, 800-542-9730
- Believe in Tomorrow Children's Foundation: www.believein tomorrow.org, 800-933-5470

Travel Assistance

- The Air Care Alliance: www.aircareall.org, 888-260-9707
- The Air Charity Network: www.aircharitynetwork.org, 877-621-7177
- Angel Flight: www.angelflightmidatlantic.org, 800-296-3797
- Corporate Angel Network: www.corpangelnetwork.org/index .htm, 866-328-1313 (for children with cancer)
- Hope Air: www.hopeair.org, 877-346-4673 (Canada only)
- Mercy Medical Airlift: www.mercymedical.org, 800-296-1217
- National Patient Travel Center: www.patienttravel.org, 800-296-1217

4

Dependent Advocate

If God didn't hesitate to put everything on the line
for us, embracing our condition and exposing
himself to the worst by sending his own Son, is
there anything else he wouldn't gladly and freely
do for us?

Romans 8:32

Hold fast to the fact that God is good and in control.
Nancy, mother of Sam who is
visually impaired, and has diabetes
and mild cerebral palsy

Many modern parents think they're in control of their child's life. Why wouldn't they? Birth control allows them to decide when their child will be born. Vaccinations prevent smallpox, polio, measles, and other childhood diseases. Antibiotics cure pediatric pneumonia, flu shots limit yearly viruses, and our country's cheap and plentiful food supply curbs malnutrition and hunger-related diseases.

Parents religiously follow the advice in the latest parenting book, convinced that by doing so their little bundles of joy will become happy and healthy kids, and eventually successful adults. For years, parents of typical children operate under the false assumption that they are in control. When their kids reach early adolescence and assert their independence, the illusion fades away.

For parents of kids with special needs, the illusion of control evaporates sooner. At the onset of symptoms and certainly after diagnosis, parents are confronted by the limits of their control over their children. As a result, their dreams and expectations change. They realize they can't make their baby well. They can't protect their child from pain. They can't predict the future. They begin wondering who is in control.

Do you remember when your illusion of control was stripped away and your questions began? *If I'm not in control of my child's life, who is? If God is in control, why did He allow this to happen to a little child? How can I trust a God who lets things like this happen?*

Those questions are a normal response to your child's diagnosis. God will not strike you dead for asking them. In fact, the Bible spotlights people who questioned God's control, or sovereignty, over their lives. Habakkuk didn't mince any words when he spoke to God: "So why don't you do something about this? Why are you silent now? This outrage! Evil men swallow up the righteous and you stand around and watch!" (Habakkuk 1:13).

If God let an Old Testament prophet ask hard questions and later made them part of His holy Scripture, then certainly He'll allow your questions, too.

If your confidence in God's sovereignty is shaky right now, don't beat yourself up. Rest assured that many parents have been where you are now, struggling with their lack of control, wrestling with

God, and eventually finding answers that led them to, or restored, their faith.

God Is in Control

When I conduct interviews with parents of kids who have special needs, I often ask this question: "What advice do you have for parents who are struggling to reconcile their child's condition with who God is?"

Their responses are surprisingly similar. Before offering advice, parents say something like, "That's a hard question." Then they share what they learned about faith while raising their children.

Colleen, whose daughter Chloe was diagnosed with Acute Lymphoblastic Leukemia (ALL) at the age of fourteen says, "I can't give answers for the mystery of God's ways. I know that a child's sickness cuts to the core of a person's belief system. I would teach parents to look for God in each day. He is faithful. He is there. He is working. He is not afraid of our doubts. I do believe God prepared us for this journey before it started and there is a purpose greater than we know."

Dan and Amy's daughter Kylie has multiple diagnoses, including autism. Dan says the answer to the question depends on people's perception of God: "If they perceive God to be like Santa, they might not be too happy about their child receiving what seems like a lump of coal."

Dan and Amy's wisdom grew out of their perception of who God is. "We both believe that God has a purpose and a perfect plan for us and our Kylie. We feel we were chosen to be Kylie's parents. God does not make mistakes, so our life is what it is supposed to be. God will give us, and Kylie, everything we need to be successful on the path He has for us."

Nancy's advice is based on what she learned after her son Sam became ill and nearly died nine hours after a normal, healthy birth:

"Hold fast to the truth that God is good and in control. He is who He says He is. God has a purpose. He is holding us."

Ellen's second child was born with Down syndrome. She explains, "I can talk about crushed dreams and hold it against God, but that's selfish. If I let go, I see God using her in lives. I'm honored to be trusted with this child."

How Can I Be Sure God Is in Control?

You may be wondering, why are those parents so sure God is in control? How did they develop such conviction? Their faith grew as they spent time in God's Word. They searched the Bible, the book that records hard questions asked of God by Habakkuk and many others. As they searched, these modern-day parents found hundreds of verses that attest to God's sovereign control over life and His compassion in good times and bad.

Colleen found comfort in a psalm that uses the word *despair*. She says the word perfectly described her emotions after Chloe's cancer diagnosis. The verse reads, "I would have despaired unless I had believed that I would see the goodness of the Lord in the land of the living" (Psalm 27:13 NASB).

A verse from Isaiah gave Dan and Amy strength as Kylie's autistic behaviors emerged. They continue to lean on the verse when Kylie acts out or has a meltdown. Isaiah 40:11 reads, "He tends his flock like a shepherd: He gathers the lambs in his arms and carries them close to his heart; he gently leads those that have young" (NIV).

Psalm 139 reminded Nancy that God was sovereignly in control of Sam's life before he was born:

> Oh yes, you shaped me first inside, then out;
>   you formed me in my mother's womb.
> I thank you, High God—you're breathtaking!
>   Body and soul, I am marvelously made!
> I worship in adoration—what a creation!

You know me inside and out,
    you know every bone in my body;
You know exactly how I was made, bit by bit,
how I was sculpted from nothing into something.
Like an open book you watched me grow from
      conception to birth;
    all the stages of my life were spread out before you,
The days of my life all prepared
    before I'd even lived one day. (vv. 13–16)

Through Scripture, God consistently assured Colleen and Nancy, Dan and Amy of His sovereignty over the lives of their children. They read about people in difficult circumstances who expressed anger and helplessness to the God who loved them in the midst of their troubles. Those examples gave them strength to cling to Him despite their own circumstances. In God's Word, they found reason to trust His plans, even when they couldn't understand them.

But these parents do more than *read* Scripture. They *pray* Scripture. Colleen wrote Psalm 27:13 and many other verses on cards she uses to pray for herself and Chloe. Amy and Dan pray the Isaiah passage, substituting Kylie's name for "the flock" and their names for "those who have young." Nancy prays Psalm 139 for Sam, asking God to continue to form and sculpt him.

If God Is in Control, Why Should I Pray?

At this point you may be thinking, if God is sovereign and so totally in control that He has known my child's days since conception, why should I pray at all? Since He's got everything covered, why bother?

Over the centuries, theologians have debated that question. As the parent of a child recently diagnosed with special needs, you don't have the time or energy to join the debate—you need immediate answers that ease your doubts and motivate you to pray. Here are two reasons from Scripture that moved me to partner with the sovereign God to pray for my son:

- Jesus tells us to pray. In fact, He commands it. He says in Matthew 6:9, "Pray very simply. Like this . . ." and then He gives His listeners an outline for prayer, which we call the Lord's Prayer. He tells us in Matthew 7:7, "Don't bargain with God. Be direct. Ask for what you need."
- Jesus, the Son of God, modeled prayer for us. The gospels recount numerous occasions when Jesus prayed. In His prayer shortly before He was arrested, He prays as He instructed the disciples to pray in Matthew 7:7: "My Father, if there is any way, get me out of this" (Matthew 26:39). Since Jesus prayed, shouldn't we?

Reasons to Pray

- Jesus tells us to pray.
- Jesus, the Son of God, prayed.
- Through prayer we advocate before God.
- Through prayer we acknowledge God's power and our weakness.

Here are two commonsense reasons for prayer that motivate me:

- We advocate for our children in health care, governmental, and educational agencies on earth. We should advocate in the spiritual realm as well. Through prayer, we can advocate before God on behalf of our children.

- Prayer is an admission of God's sovereignty, His rule over our lives. When we pray, we admit our weakness and limited vision and submit to His greater power and insight. We are advocates who acknowledge our dependence on the faithful God who sent His Son to save those who love Him.

How Do I Pray to a Sovereign God?

God loves to honor our prayers when they are consistent with His will. But discerning His will and praying according to it is hard work. Once again, His Word is a powerful tool to guide our efforts. We can use Scripture to pray in God's will. He makes this promise in Isaiah 55:11: "So will the words that come out of my mouth not come back empty-handed. They'll do the work I sent them to do, they'll complete the assignment I gave them." According to that verse, God has reasons for every word in the Bible. When His Word resonates with what's happening in our lives, when His promises echo the desires of our hearts, we can confidently pray Scripture back to Him. He will use our prayers, offered in faith, to change us while completing His plans for our children.

The plan may be a successful treatment. It may be teaching a child to live with a special need. Or it could be losing a child far too early. Still, in every circumstance and situation, even when our hearts are breaking, we can trust God to take His words offered back through our prayers, and complete the work He sent them to do.

Because praying Scripture often feels awkward at first, you may want to use the prayer guide "Thirty Prayers of Dependence" in appendix A to get started. The selected Scripture verses speak about God's sovereignty and compassion toward those who depend on Him. Following each verse is an example of how to pray through it.

As you grow accustomed to praying Scripture, try personalizing passages for yourself and your family. As God's Word becomes familiar to you, you may want to create your own prayer guide.

How Can I Become a Dependent Advocate?

If you trust that God has a plan for your child, then His sovereignty will be a great comfort to you on your special needs journey. You will have confidence to move beyond diagnosis into your child's future. Why? Because the future isn't in your frail hands. It's in the hands of a capable, sovereign God who loves you and your child.

You can depend on Him to show you how to be your child's voice in prayer. He will answer those prayers through His Word, the recommendations of professionals and experts, the counsel of godly people, and the advice of parents who have had experiences similar to yours. He will answer by shaping you into an effective, resourceful, dependent advocate.

The sovereign God is with you. What a relief to be free from the illusion of human control!

Dear Sovereign God, in light of our child's diagnosis, it is hard to believe you are in control. If I didn't know you were a parent who watched His Son suffer on my behalf, I wouldn't trust you at all. I'm clinging to the assurance that you know what will happen next. When my faith grows weak and I doubt your control, will you hold me? Will you hold on for me?

If you are still wrestling with the issues of God's sovereignty and goodness, these two books will address many of your questions: The Problem of Pain *by C. S. Lewis and* If God Is Good: Faith in the Midst of Suffering and Evil *by Randy Alcorn. Both authors explore Scripture from the perspective of people in the midst of suffering and loss.*

Take Time to Reflect

Resources

- "Thirty Prayers of Dependence" in appendix A
- Randy Alcorn, *If God Is Good: Faith in the Midst of Suffering and Evil* (Multnomah, 2009).
- C. S. Lewis, *The Problem of Pain* (HarperOne, 2001).

Hospital Life

From Confused to Confident

5

Confident in the Halls

For this is what the Lord says: "I will extend peace
to her like a river, and the wealth of nations like a
flooding stream; you will nurse and be carried on
her arm and dandled on her knees. As a mother
comforts her child, so will I comfort you."

Isaiah 66:12–13 (NIV)

Be friendly. The staff is on your team and wants
what's best for your child. They are not perfect but
are working hard to be helpful and ease the pain.

Colleen, mother of Chloe,
a survivor of acute lymphoblastic leukemia (ALL)

Melody's pregnancy was uneventful for the first twenty-five weeks. Then tests showed signs of preeclampsia. She was admitted to the hospital immediately. Two days later, she and her husband, Ryan, welcomed their daughter Reagan into the world. She weighed one pound, four ounces and spent 112 days in the neonatal intensive care unit (NICU). A year and a half later, sister Kenady spent seventeen days in NICU after her birth at thirty-three weeks, weighing four pounds, eleven ounces. Nearly four years later, brother Jaxson arrived at twenty-seven weeks. He weighed two pounds, three and a half ounces. After 110 days in NICU, Jaxson came home with Ryan and Melody.

Duration of hospital stays: 239 days with three single birth newborns

●

Kylie was born via emergency caesarean section. Due to low birth weight, she was unable to maintain her body temperature and was placed in a warmer. Because her birth mother had gestational diabetes, Kylie endured foot pricks for several days. Meanwhile, Kylie's adoptive parents, Dan and Amy, camped out in the waiting room. The hospital eventually downgraded Kylie's status from patient to boarder, requiring the family to care for their baby in the less than ideal conditions of the waiting room. Finally, Dan and Amy were allowed to take their new daughter to a nearby hotel and care for her there. Years later, memories of their treatment in the hospital create anxiety for their family.

Duration of hospital stay: 4 days

●

Chloe was diagnosed with acute lymphoblastic leukemia (ALL) one week after a routine blood test revealed an abnormally low platelet count. Colleen, Chloe's mom, drove her daughter to the hospital for her first round of chemo in October, shortly after Chloe's fourteenth birthday. Two and a half years later, Chloe completed her final round of standard chemo treatment. At the age of sixteen, she was cancer free.

Duration of hospital stays: 59 days over two and a half years

●

Jason and Nancy greeted their son, Sam, after a normal pregnancy and delivery. But nine hours later, for some unknown reason, Sam's condition deteriorated. Two days later, he was rushed to a hospital across town and placed on an extracorporeal membrane oxygenation (ECMO) machine, which mimicked the natural function of Sam's heart and lungs so his body could rest and heal. Gradually, his condition stabilized and he was weaned off the machine, but he had suffered a brain bleed due to the ECMO treatment. The bleed resulted in several conditions—visual impairment, posthemorrhagic hydrocephalus, diabetes insipidus, and mild cerebral palsy (CP)—requiring more surgeries, procedures, and treatments.

Duration of hospital stays: 58 days from birth to six months

From Confused to Confident

Long or short. Scheduled or emergency. Routine or unexpected. No matter the circumstances, kids and hospital stays are not a natural combination, and parenting a hospitalized child is beyond the scope of the average dad or mom's responsibilities. Moms want to paint the baby's nursery, not decorate an NICU cubicle. Dads want to ride bikes with their sons and daughters, not monitor IV drips and breathing treatments. Parents want to make their children's owies better, not hand their kids over to masked strangers who will hurt them.

If your child is alive because of hospital intervention, in the quiet depths of your soul—beneath the tidal wave of diagnosis, the flood of emotions unleashed by medical procedures and treatments, and the stream of caregivers—you are grateful for the medical care your child is receiving. Yet being grateful doesn't make the hospital any less confusing. Nor does it make you feel confident about how to parent in such a strange environment.

For the duration of the hospital stay, your child needs a confident, loving parent. In the next four chapters, you'll learn about resources and strategies designed to decrease your confusion and increase your confidence.

What Is Patient- and Family-Centered Care?

University of Iowa Children's Hospital defines patient- and family-centered care as "an approach to the planning, delivery, and evaluation of health care that is grounded in mutually beneficial partnerships among children, their families, and health care professionals."

Tap into What the Hospital Offers

Most children's hospital personnel know that supportive, attentive parents are good for their pint-sized charges. Therefore, patient- and family-centered care is now the standard for hospitals that treat kids. With family-centered care comes a variety of hospital services. Your child's primary nurse, a social worker, or a child life specialist should acquaint you with services during check in. If that doesn't happen, look for a directory in your child's hospital room or check the hospital's website until you can ask for more information.

For brief hospital stays, the services described below are sufficient. For lengthy or repeated hospitalizations, parents can access additional assistance through the patient- and family-centered care department (see chapters 6 and 7).

Programs vary from place to place, but the following services are standard in university and children's hospitals.

Regular Inpatient Services: If your child will be in a regular inpatient room, you can expect:

- A fold-out bed with bedding so you can spend the night in your child's room.
- Access to the floor's galley kitchen for occasional snacks and drinks.

- Bathroom and shower facilities.
- A visit from a child life specialist to educate your child about upcoming procedures.
- Internet access via a laptop and/or a public computer.
- A map of the hospital and/or directions to the cafeteria, coffee shop, and chapel.
- An explanation of parking locations, rules, and fees.
- A visiting hours schedule for other family members.
- Access to a playroom and activities for kids.
- Access to child-appropriate TV channels, DVDs, and video games.
- A cafeteria schedule and perhaps a menu.

Intensive Care Services: NICU and pediatric intensive care unit (PICU) services vary from hospital to hospital. Depending on the unit's layout and the fragility of your child's condition, the following may be available:

- Individual NICU or PICU rooms where parents can stay with children day and night.
- A NICU or PICU ward parents can visit day or night, with nearby private sleeping rooms or a large waiting area for cat-naps.
- Hospital meals delivered for nursing mothers or parents of children in critical condition.

If you're at a regional or general hospital rather than a university or children's hospital, patient- and family-centered care may not be standard operating procedure. In that case, you will need to educate the people caring for your child. Start by politely asking for what you need in order to stay in your child's room. If your request is denied, calmly and firmly ask to speak to a supervisor or department head. If that doesn't work, call your doctor. Stay calm, but keep asking until your request is granted. Your child needs the security of your presence. You must be present to be your child's voice, so don't give up.

Tap into an Emotional Support Network

When your child is in the hospital, you need more than a fold-out cot next to a hospital bed. You need more than showers, food, and a high-speed Internet connection. You need emotional support, a network of people who will lift you up when you can't stand alone.

Veteran hospital parents know that vulnerable moments come at the most inopportune and unexpected times, usually when they're alone and tired. They know it's important to have a support network in place beforehand so they aren't defenseless when the down times come. To build a multifaceted support network, utilize several groups.

Hospital Network: Immediately tap into available hospital personnel. Hospital chaplains and social workers will listen to your concerns. They will also point you to professionals who can meet your needs.

Take advantage of the built-in support network of parents on your pediatric floor. The other parents know what you're going through because they're going through it, too. Your fears are their fears. Your emotions are their emotions. So reach out to them. Visit with them in the halls. Encourage them to talk about their families while your kids pal around in the playroom. Ask them for advice. Connect with them so that when you feel vulnerable—in the middle of the night when you can't sleep, while you wait to hear news of your child's surgery, or when the doctor shares unwelcome news— someone will be sitting beside you, holding your hand.

Personal Network: Though hospitals provide professional support and a ready cadre of parents, your most effective network will be the people who know you best: family, friends, neighbors, church family, and coworkers. To maintain a strong personal network, good

Three Ways to Streamline Communication with Family and Friends

- Assign a communications coordinator to make and screen calls.
- Set up a free website at CarePages or CaringBridge.
- Use social networks like Facebook or Twitter.

communication is essential. Thanks to modern technology, communication devices are often at your fingertips no matter where you are.

In fact, your biggest problem may be too much communication. The ring of a cell phone during the doctor's rounds creates an unwanted distraction. During nap time for your child (and you), it can make you crazy. The combination of an overwhelmed parent and an overflowing e-mail inbox can be downright ugly.

To avoid these sanity-stressers, try implementing some of the tips below. They'll keep you sane and your support network informed and empowered.

- Ask one tech savvy friend or family member to coordinate communication. Call or e-mail a daily status report to the coordinator, along with emergency updates when necessary. The coordinator then passes the information to others.
- Facilitate communication with CaringBridge or CarePages. These two websites provide free web pages for patients and their families. You and child can tell your story, write updates, make prayer requests, and post photos. Friends and family can leave messages to be read when convenient. Their websites are listed at the end of this chapter.
- Share information quickly on Twitter and Facebook. (If you're concerned about privacy issues, stick with CaringBridge and CarePages. They provide safeguards to limit public access.)

Tap into the Source of Your Confidence

Remember, you are your child's voice during the hospital stay. In every situation, with every person you meet, your tone of voice influences your child's care and treatment.

Yet remaining calm and confident can be a challenge, especially when you're sleep-deprived, stressed, emotional, and confused. Sam's mom, Nancy, describes the conundrum well: "You have to advocate for your child—at times, firmly—but learning how to do that and maintain a Christlike witness can be challenging."

To meet the challenge when you're stressed, lean on this promise from Scripture:

> For this is what the Lord says: "I will extend peace to her like a river, and the wealth of nations like a flooding stream; you will nurse and be carried on her arm and dandled on her knees. As a mother comforts her child, so will I comfort you." (Isaiah 66:12–13 NIV)

This verse says God is *your* parent. He is caring for you while you care for your child. When you understand that promise, and trust your heavenly Parent to be the most powerful member of your patient- and family-centered care team, you can be a calm and confident, Christlike witness.

When you're sleep-deprived and stressed, scared and lonely, close your eyes. Picture yourself being carried in God's arms, dandled on His knees. Then open your eyes and look at the people in your support system—family, friends, and hospital staff. They are God's instruments of peace and comfort. Cry out to them. God will use them to comfort you.

Dear Father, the hospital world is strange and foreign. I am out of my element, unsure of what to do and say. Grant me a spirit of calm in this unfamiliar place. Make me aware of the people you've sent to strengthen me when I feel vulnerable. Make me aware of the people who can improve my child's care.

What needs to be done to improve my child's level of care? How will I phrase my requests to be both firm and Christlike? What can I say and do to show the staff how their efforts and skill are appreciated?

Take Time to Reflect

Resources

Family-Centered Care Information

- Learn more about patient- and family-centered care at your hospital by typing the phrase into the search box at their website.
- National Institute of Patient- and Family-Centered Care (IPFCC): http://www.ipfcc.org/

Online Communication Tools

- CarePages: www.carepages.com
- CaringBridge: www.caringbridge.org
- Baby Home Pages: www.babyhomepages.net

6

Confident with the Help

Each time my son was admitted to the hospital, I had the sense of entering an eerie, foreign land. The doors shut and we were trapped in a kingdom with halls instead of roads and elevators instead of cars. The kingdom's citizens dressed in color-coded scrubs, latex gloves, puffy paper hats and slippers, face masks, and white coats accessorized by stethoscopes and blood-pressure cuffs.

When I wasn't reassuring Allen, I often felt lost and disoriented. Hospital workers rotated in and out of his room, and I had trouble sorting through the people involved in his care regime. I wasted precious time and energy asking the wrong people the right questions. I asked nurses questions only the doctor could answer, therapists questions only a nurse could answer, and nurses' assistants questions only the therapist could answer.

Documenting Allen's care was an exercise in futility since I wasn't sure who did what or what they were doing. Without a medical dictionary, I couldn't make sense of the jargon used by health care workers. I was in a foreign land without a guide to interpret the language or explain the idiosyncrasies of hospital culture.

Thankfully, the recent patient- and family-centered care movement has made positive changes in hospitals for parents and kids. Many university and children's hospitals give parents a printed guide of hospital services when children are admitted. Some guides even have a glossary of common medical terms. If your hospital doesn't have such a resource, use this chapter as your guide in a strange and foreign land.

Who's on Your Child's Care Team?

The number of people directly involved in your child's hospital care may surprise you. The personnel will vary from one hospital to another, but every health care team should include these categories of care.

Physician Care

More than one physician will care for your child. The more complicated your child's case, the greater number of physicians will be involved. Many divide their time between clinic and hospital. They administer some care themselves, such as surgery, but prescribe much of it for therapists and nurses to perform.

Specialists and Doctors: In large hospitals, doctors specialize in a chosen area. In children's hospitals, doctors have additional training in pediatrics within their specialty area. Normally, the specialist sees your child in the clinic before hospitalization, during daily rounds, and again in the clinic after hospitalization.

Attending Physicians: This type of doctor, also called the staff doctor, is responsible for your child's overall care during the hospital stay. The attending physician examines your child, monitors daily progress, plans care, and oversees treatment. He or she will join the specialist during rounds, and may be more visible through the day.

Fellows and Residents: These doctors have completed medical school and are licensed physicians receiving specialized training, usually at university hospitals. They often accompany the specialist and attending physician on rounds. Fellows have completed their residency. Residents are scheduled so at least one is on duty in the hospital twenty-four hours a day, seven days a week. Therefore, they may have close contact with you and your child.

Only doctors, attending physicians, fellows, and residents can prescribe care, including changes in medicines, therapies, procedures, and tests, so it is important to have care questions ready when the doctor arrives. (Large hospitals may also employ physician assistants and nurse practitioners who can prescribe care on a limited basis or under the supervision of a licensed doctor.)

Nursing Care

Nurses administer care directly to patients, so they spend more time with them than doctors do. Training levels dictate what each nurse can and can't do.

Nurse Managers: Nurse managers lead the staff in their unit. They can help parents resolve problems and concerns. An assistant nurse manager supports the nurse manager.

Registered Nurses (RN): RNs are responsible for all general nursing care and for educating patients and their families. If your child has a "primary nurse," he or she is an RN.

Licensed Practical Nurses (LPN): Some hospitals assign an LPN to your child on each shift to assist the RN.

Nursing Assistants: A nursing assistant is assigned to your child on each shift to support the nursing team.

Nursing Unit Clerks: Clerks provide clerical support for each unit and communicate patient- and family-care requests to the care team. They handle the paperwork for patient admissions, transfers, and discharges. They can also answer many nonmedical questions.

Remember, nurses administer treatment, but can't prescribe it. If you feel a change in treatment is needed before the doctor's next scheduled visit (such as new medication or removal of an IV), tell the nurse. He or she can phone the doctor, explain the situation, and ask the doctor for new orders. Once they are received, the changes can be made.

Therapists

Depending on your child's needs, one or more of the following therapists may work with your child.

Respiratory Therapists (RT): These therapists evaluate and treat patients with breathing problems. They administer oxygen, monitor ventilators, and educate parents and patients about equipment and ongoing respiratory care.

Physical Therapists (PT): The PT evaluates the patient's development and functional skills, and then helps children learn to use their bodies through exercise.

Occupational Therapists (OT): The OT assesses a child's motor, sensory, cognitive, perceptual, and psychosocial development. He or she then helps children gain maximum independence in daily care, play, and school activities.

If you have concerns about therapy, discuss them with the appropriate therapist. In cooperation with the nurses, they can contact doctor and ask for new orders, if necessary.

The Rest of the Team

Other important members of your child's health care team are phlebotomists, child life specialists, and social workers.

Phlebotomists: These specially trained staff members draw blood for lab tests.

Child Life Specialists: These wonderful people help patients and families adjust to the hospital. They are trained to meet kids' special needs during hospitalization. They help children and parents understand medical issues and prepare kids for procedures, often allowing them to explore real medical equipment. They comfort kids during procedures and tests. They also arrange normal play activities for children convalescing in their rooms.

Social Workers: Social workers guide families through physical, emotional, and financial issues related to a child's illness. They are available to assist parents during hospitalization, treatment, discharge, and return to school. They connect families to financial and social service resources, as well as coordinating therapy and support services provided by community and educational agencies.

What Support Services Can Help Us?

With so many people involved in your child's care, it must be hard to imagine that more services are available. But they are. The following support services are standard in hospitals.

- *Spiritual Services:* Hospitals have chaplains, sometimes available twenty-four hours a day. Some hospitals offer weekly services on a regular basis.
- *Grief Services:* Emotional support is available for families dealing with lost dreams, not just the death of a child. They may

offer counseling, reading materials, and mementos to document the importance of a child's life.

- *Pain and Palliative Care Services:* These services are available for children who face chronic or debilitating pain, or a terminal diagnosis.
- *Peer-to-Peer Support:* Some hospitals have programs that connect families with similar experiences through one-on-one meetings or group support for parents, children, and siblings.
- *Patient Representatives:* Sometimes called patient advocates, these staff members provide family support and assistance with concerns, questions, and issues about your child's hospital stay.

Keep in mind that your hospital may offer additional services not on this list.

How Should I Advocate with the Care Team?

First, remember that you are a valuable member of the care team. No one knows your child quite like you do. Your expertise will assist the others in providing the best possible care for your child. Be confident, firm, and gracious when communicating with the team members.

Next, be proactive about the make up of the care team. When you find highly skilled professionals who relate well to your child, ask to have them permanently assigned to your child's care team. When Kenady, Ryan and Melody's second child, was born prematurely in the same hospital as their first preemie daughter, they requested, and were assigned, the same primary nurse. "We pushed to get her," Melody explains, "because she knew us so well."

In a care conference, the members of the child's health care team (which includes the parent) sit down together to discuss the child's care. Anyone on the team can call a care conference to discuss progress or breakthroughs, coordinate services, or troubleshoot prob-

How to Foster Care Team Unity

1. Develop good working relationships with team members.
2. Talk openly and constructively.
3. Respect the knowledge, skills, experiences, and qualities of other team members.
4. Make your family's background, culture, and interests known. They are important.
5. Do your best to work out differences and problems.
6. Pursue excellent outcomes for your child.

Adapted from the University of Iowa's Coordinated Care Manual

lems. You can also call for a conference if you have a concern. The nurse manager, social worker, or child life specialist can assist you in starting the process. Write down your concerns beforehand so you can state them calmly and confidently in the meeting. Keep asking questions until you feel the treatment and support your child's condition requires is in place.

If one parent can't attend the care conference because of work or other obligations, borrow this technique from Kenady's mom and dad. Melody attended the conference in person, and doctors phoned Ryan via Skype so he could participate, too.

What If a Problem Can't Be Resolved?

If you have concerns about your child's level of care, do all you can to communicate and work with the members of the care team to solve problems. If your concerns aren't heard or resolved, you will need to talk with the patient representative on your child's care team. In the absence of a patient representative, contact the hospital's patient representative program or patients' rights department. To locate them, check the hospital website, or call the hospital switchboard operator and ask to be transferred to their office.

If your concern is still not dealt with appropriately, contact your state's health care regulatory department. The Hospice Patients Alliance provides an online directory of state regulatory agencies at www.hospicepatients.org/stadrss.html. You can also report concerns to the Joint Commission at www.jointcommission.org.

Will I Ever Feel at Home in This Foreign Land?

To be honest, the hospital never felt like home, though we visited it frequently during Allen's first five years. But our confusion lessened with each stay, and the hospital kingdom felt less foreign. The same thing will happen with you. As you learn the lingo and routines, you'll become a confident advocate and caregiver. You'll come to believe what the hospital personnel already know: You are most valuable person on your child's care team. You're the parent. That makes you the number-one expert about your child.

Dear Father, thank you for the doctors, nurses, therapists, and others on my child's care team. Settle your Spirit on the entire team. Unify the care we provide. Mark it with the grace only you can provide.

Who should be enlisted for my child's care team? What questions do I have for the care team? How can I prepare for care team meetings so I feel confident when attending them?

Take Time to Reflect

Resources

General Resources

- Visit the hospital's website to identify and locate available services and contact information for specific hospital staff members.
- Skype: www.skype.com

Complaint or Grievance Resources

- The Hospice Patients Alliance: www.hospicepatients.org /stadrss.html
- Joint Commission: www.jointcommission.org

7

Confident at the Bedside

I will always show you where to go. I'll give you a full
life in the emptiest of places—firm muscles, strong
bones. You'll be like a well-watered garden, a gur-
gling spring that never runs dry.

Isaiah 58:11

If you'll be in the hospital for any length of time,
bring comforts from home—favorite blankets,
stuffed animals, and toys.

Lisa Fox, Child Life Specialist,
Des Moines Mercy Hospital

As a young child, my daughter interpreted everything she heard
literally. One day when Anne was six, my hair was in a French braid,
and at supper I said, "I had lots of compliments on my hair today."

Anne studied my head for a long minute, and then declared, "Mommy, I don't see anything on your hair." Somehow, my husband, son, and I managed not to laugh.

A few weeks later, the local frog population went into kamikaze mode, hopping onto roads and driveways in droves. When we climbed out of the car after church one Sunday, a flattened frog graced our driveway. "Oh, look." I pointed. "An ex-frog."

Anne stared intently at the critter. "But Mommy,"—she looked up, her expression puzzled—"I don't see an X on that frog."

Ah, Anne. As she matured, her thinking became less concrete, better able to grasp and interpret abstract language and concepts. Now an adult, she no longer looks for compliments on hair or a frog marked with an X. Some days I miss seeing the world through her younger eyes.

A child's view of the world is different from yours and mine. Imagine how confusing a first encounter with the hospital world must be to a kid. If it feels like a foreign land to you, it must seem like outer space to a child.

There are strange sights, sounds, smells, and funny tasting food—if doctors allow your child to eat. A stranger says, "Here's your room," but the room doesn't look at all like the bedroom at home. Then the stranger says, "Put on these pajamas," and they're the weirdest pajamas ever.

Another stranger walks in and says, "I need to feel your tummy," and reaches under the pajamas. But your child knows strangers aren't supposed to touch kids, especially not under their clothes. Mom and Dad say, "It's okay. Do what she says." What's a kid supposed to do in such a crazy place? How can you stay sane for your child?

Preparing Your Child for What's Ahead

As a parent, you are your child's bedside guide and interpreter in this crazy place. Child life specialists and others may also help your child adjust to strange surroundings, but you can do the best job of preparing your child. You are with your child more than anyone else, and because you know your child so well, you can anticipate reactions and offer comfort.

Of course, the preparation varies depending on the child's age. Child life specialists recommend the following strategies.

Birth to age two: In this age group, the focus is on preparing parents for what will happen so they know where to stand and what to do. Parents should be present whenever possible, but not participate in procedures that cause pain. Instead, the parents should be allowed to "rescue" the child afterward and provide comfort.

Ages three to four: Preparation for preschoolers should begin a few days before hospitalization. Parents should concentrate on communicating accurately, saying, "*You* need to go to the hospital" instead of "*We* need to go." When the day arrives, avoid asking, "Are you ready to go to the hospital?" because the child has to go, whether he's ready or not. Instead, allow the child appropriate control by asking, "Do you want to take your blue pajamas or the green ones?" Use "soft language" when explaining hospital procedures and think about how your words sound to a child who interprets language concretely. See "Hospital Lingo vs. Soft Language" for common misinterpretations.

Ages five to twelve: School-aged children benefit most from hands-on medical play. Child life specialists or nurses in a pediatric clinic will allow children to touch and wear an anesthesia mask. Kids can dress in a gown, cap, mask, and slippers. They play with a syringe (minus the needle, of course), use a stethoscope, and experiment with a tongue depressor and thermometer. While the child plays, the adult explains how the equipment is used and what will happen.

Ages twelve to eighteen: Adolescents like to talk about what will happen. They want to be treated like an adult. They should be encouraged to ask questions and talk about how they feel.

Hospital Lingo (HL) vs. Soft Language (SL)

HL: The doctor will give you some "dye." Child thinks, "To make me die?"

SL: "The doctor will put some medicine in the tube that will help her see your insides more clearly."

HL: Urine. Child thinks, "You're in?"

SL: Use the child's familiar term.

HL: I.C.U. Child thinks, "I see you?"

SL: Explain what each letter means—Intensive Care Unit.

HL: Stretcher. Child thinks, "Stretch her? Stretch who? Why?"

SL: Say instead "bed on wheels."

HL: "They're going to put you to sleep." Child thinks, "The vet put my dog to sleep and she never woke up."

SL: "They're going to give you sleepy medicine."

Entertaining a Hospitalized Child

Whenever Allen was on the mend in the hospital, he grew increasingly bored and restless. Keeping him quiet and entertained required creativity and resourcefulness. The hospital playrooms, library, craft rooms, and television in his room helped, but they weren't tailored to his specific likes and interests.

Over the years, we learned to ask family and friends to create care packages. They loved the request because it gave them a tangible way to help. They knew his tastes and sense of humor, so they picked out books, movies, and CDs guaranteed to please him. Knowing that friends from home were thinking of him was a huge encouragement to Allen and to us.

When people ask what they can do to make your child's hospital stay easier, request care packages and include suggestions for what to put in it. Depending on the age and interests of your child, ask for the following:

- *Art supplies:* Markers, crayons, coloring books, drawing paper, scissors, glue sticks, paper dolls
- *Hands-on supplies:* Silly Putty, Play-Doh (along with a small rolling pin and cookie cutters), cat's cradle instructions and string, small weaving loom and cloth loops for making pot holders
- *Reading material:* kids' magazines, favorite books, books by favorite authors, joke books, books in a series
- *Techno goodies:* DVDs, CDs, iTunes gift certificates, video games
- *Food:* favorite snacks and drinks, gift cards to nearby favorite restaurants
- *Small toys:* Matchbox cars or Hot Wheels, Slinkies, Polly Pocket–type toys, Legos, snap together models, jigsaw puzzles
- *Card games:* Uno, Skip-Bo, Go Fish, Old Maid, Phase 10, Crazy 8s
- *Travel-sized board games:* Candyland, Chutes and Ladders, Connect Four, Checkers, Sorry, Chess, Monopoly

Taking Care of Yourself

So far this chapter has discussed how to make your child comfortable in the hospital. Now let's talk about how to keep you healthy and strong enough to stay by your child's side. Before the discussion begins, repeat these words:

Taking care of myself is not selfish. It is essential.
Taking care of myself is not selfish. It is essential.
Taking care of myself is not selfish. It is essential.

If you have ruby slippers, feel free to click them now, but the chances of you returning to a farmhouse in Kansas are slim.

I learned the importance of self-care after indulging in an episode of what one hospital mom calls "Mama Tiger mode." My Mama Tiger incident occurred when Allen was hospitalized at age four for a Nissen fundoplication, a surgery that builds a valve into the stomach. Because my husband, Hiram, was less than a year into a new job and couldn't get time off, he visited the hospital in the evening, stayed overnight at the Ronald McDonald House, and went to work from there.

Allen and I were together 24/7, starting the evening before surgery. The nurse helped Allen settle in, and then showed me how to fold out the recliner into a bed. Soon after, Allen and I hit the sack. Sometime in the night, cold air started blasting from the vent above my bed. It woke me, but unwilling to bother anyone, I suffered in silence.

The next morning, my ear crackled and popped like a bowl of Rice Krispies. I ignored it, like any good Mama Tiger with a cub going under the knife would. In the surgery waiting room, my ear started to ache. But I wasn't going anywhere—what if the doctor came to talk to me while I was off having my ear examined? What kind of mother would do that?

The pain mounted through Allen's stint in recovery and his rocky adjustment to PICU. By the time my husband arrived, the pain was so bad my whole head hurt when I swallowed. Later the emergency room doctor scolded me for letting the ear infection go so long, and then laid a hand on my shoulder. "I know you didn't want to leave your little boy, but he needs you healthy. Who will take care of him if you're sick? Next time, tell someone what's wrong so we can help."

She was right, of course. Instead of prowling around the hospital room lair, protecting my young cub, I should have taken care of myself. After all, we were in a hospital full of doctors. Surely one could have come to Allen's room, checked my ear, and prescribed antibiotics.

Hospital parents can easily fall victim to Mama or Papa Tiger behavior. It happened to Diana, who created the term when her son went through months of procedures and surgery to correct the effects of Hirschsprung's disease. One night, after a nonstop week of watching over her cub, she was exhausted. Sam was finally asleep. Diana was sure her head had barely hit the pillow before a phlebotomist knocked on the door and identified herself.

"I flew out of the bed and met her at the door. In no uncertain terms, I told her Sam had just gotten to sleep and she'd have to come some other time for the blood draw. I backed the poor woman out of the room and shut the door," Diana remembers. "Then I looked at the clock. It was four hours later than I'd thought."

Oops!

Taming Your Inner Tiger

To avoid biting the heads off innocent workers at your hospital, you must be proactive about your physical and emotional self-care. Here are some tiger-taming strategies recommended by other hospital parents.

- Trust your spouse to stay in the room overnight on alternate nights. That way, you each get eight hours of uninterrupted sleep every other night.
- If you're a single parent, or your spouse can't alternate nights, ask a close friend or relative to stay with your child for a few hours each afternoon. Then, go take a nap in the Ronald McDonald House or a hospital sleeping room.
- Find out if the hospital offers free chair massages or other perks and take advantage of them.
- Exercise every day. Walk laps in the hall while your child naps, or take your child with you in a wheelchair. Use a

stroller or a wagon for walks outside. Take the stairs instead of the elevator. If the neighborhood is safe, walk instead of drive from the Ronald McDonald House to the hospital.

- Eat fresh fruits, vegetables, and other healthy food whenever you can. A constant diet of junk food (an easy habit to fall into with vending machines nearby and the cafeteria far away) will further stress your body.
- Bring your hobby with you. I learned to pack needlework projects. Allen liked to watch the pictures take shape.
- Have fun. Watch old television comedies. Invite some friends for a movie and popcorn night. Read joke books.
- Ask your friends and family to send you a care package.

Care Packages for Adults

- Puzzle books: Sudoku, crosswords, word finds
- Books and magazines: Ask for books by laugh-out-loud authors like P. G. Wodehouse, Janet Evanovich, Patrick McManus, and Erma Bombeck.
- DVDs: Ask for your favorite comedies.
- Hobby supplies: kits for cross-stitch, scrapbooking, or other hobbies
- Comfort items: fleece blankets, pillows, slippers, comfy pajamas
- Food and drink: gourmet tea bags, spiced apple cider mixes, instant cocoa packets, healthy snacks, gift cards to nearby restaurants or coffee shops, rolls of quarters for vending machines
- Encouragement: personal notes and Bible verses

Pediatric social worker Janelle Holst Kamba gives this advice: "Couples should take time out for each other. Each parent should be allowed time away from the hospital and their sick child to focus on themselves. When offers are made for assistance, take them. Ask someone to sit with your child at the hospital while you have a date night or go home to take a long bath." She also encourages parents to take advantage of professional services at the hospital: "The hospital social worker and clergy can provide counseling to individuals and couples. If needed, referrals can also be made to outside agencies that provide similar services. Don't be afraid to ask for what you need."

Surviving the Hospital Stay

Taking care of your hospitalized child is hard, draining work that lasts all day and all night. The job requires seeing the hospital with the eyes of a child and responding to it with the stamina and creativity of an adult. Your ability to care for your child is influenced by the quality of your self-care. So don't feel guilty about taking a few minutes each day to implement one or two of the suggestions in this chapter to meet your physical and emotional needs.

When your inner spirit cries out for attention, move on to chapter 8, which is packed with ideas about how to stay spiritually strong and grateful during your child's stay in this foreign land.

Father, if the hospital is a foreign land to me, it must seem like a different planet to my child. Give me a heart to anticipate my child's questions and fears. Give me patience to listen to and answer questions. Show me when I need rest. Provide people I can trust to care for my child so I can take a break now and then.

How can I calm my child's fears? How can I change hospital talk into kid language? Who do I trust to care for my child when I need rest? How can we have fun while we are here?

Take Time to Reflect

Resources

Children's Stress Relief

- National Child Traumatic Stress Network: www.nctsnet.org. Pull down the "Trauma Types" menu at the top of the page and select "Medical Trauma." Click on "Pediatric Medical Traumatic Stress Toolkit for Health Care Providers" to access a download with tips on how to reduce stress in children.
- Peter A. Levine and Maggie Kline, *Trauma-Proofing Your Kids* (North Atlantic Books, 2008).

Parents' Stress Relief

- Amy Baskin and Heather Fawcett, *More Than a Mom: Living a Full and Balanced Life When Your Child Has Special Needs* (Woodbine House, 2006).
- Check your hospital's website or print directory for services available to parents.

8

Confident in Prayer

> Listen, God, I'm calling at the top of my lungs: "Be good to me! Answer me!" When my heart whispered, "Seek God," my whole being replied, "I'm seeking him!"
>
> Psalm 27:7–8

> Sam's hospitalization was the turning point in my faith journey. I learned what it meant to pray without ceasing. There was no line between my thoughts and my prayers.
>
> Diana, mother of Sam, who had surgery for Hirschsprung's disease at seven weeks of age

Ryan is a man who prefers to follow Christ by being a witness instead of openly talking about his faith. "I don't preach, I teach, because to me there's a big difference," he explains when he and his wife, Melody, talk about the premature births and hospitalizations of their children, Reagan, Kenady, and Jaxson. But when he describes his kids' NICU stays, he has to mention his faith. During those days, his faith became real. During those days, he learned to live what he professed to believe.

Before daughter Reagan's risky heart valve surgery four days after her birth, Ryan made the choice to release his daughter into God's hands. "I told Him, 'I'm ready to let go of Reagan and leave you in control.'" Ryan raised his eyebrows. "That's not me."

In her book *Walking on Water*, Madeleine L'Engle described how God assured her of His presence when her nine-year-old granddaughter Lena was hit by a truck and critically injured. That night, far from home and unable to return for several days, L'Engle opened her travel prayer book to the evening's psalm and found a picture of Lena and her baby brother, taken only a few weeks before. Then a card fell out, one given to her years before, and she read these words spoken by John of the Cross: "One act of thanksgiving made when things go wrong is worth a thousand when things go well."

For several days, until she could get home and see her hospitalized granddaughter, L'Engle gave thanks for her children, her grandchildren, and for Lena's nine years of life. She said, "That gift of the card falling out of my prayer book when it did was one of the greatest gifts I have ever received. It made me affirm to myself that God is in control, that ultimately all shall be well, no matter what."

Recognizing God at work isn't easy, especially in the hospital, and neither is trusting God's control in an environment where you feel powerless. Madeline L'Engle recognized God and was able to rest in His control because she was equipped to do so. Without proper preparation and necessary tools, she would have wrung her hands and paced nervously. Instead, she opened her prayer book and found God waiting to speak to her.

I wasn't as well-prepared for our first hospital adventure as L'Engle. My training began with Allen's birth. Lack of control smacked me in the face when our twelve-hour-old baby was life-flighted to a hospital

750 miles away. Sure, Hiram and I had grown up in church and believed in God. But this was the first time we realized our helplessness, our utter dependence on the God we called Savior and Lord. That afternoon, my husband and I did the only thing left to us. We prayed, releasing our child who we'd held for only a few moments into the care of God, his Creator.

My trust in God's control was repeatedly tested over the next few years. At first, I did more hand-wringing and pacing than praying and trusting. Gradually, God taught me to recognize His hand at work in Allen's life, both at home and in the hospital. Slowly, faith replaced my fear.

Special Training Regime

Each of our son's trips to the hospital honed my ability to recognize God's voice. He first spoke through Allen's primary NICU nurse, who lavished love on our baby when we couldn't be with him. Eight weeks later, our son quit breathing while I nursed him. After my husband revived him and we rode to the hospital by ambulance, God spoke through a nurse on the pediatric floor. She just happened to be from my hometown. When Allen was a toddler, God spoke with the gentle voice and kind eyes of the gastrointestinal physician Allen dubbed his "buddy doctor."

Between hospital stays, God continued to equip me. The Holy Spirit brought friends into our lives who listened to our questions: What kind of God allows babies to suffer? Why doesn't He heal our son? What purpose could He have in all this?

Our friends answered the questions when they could. When they didn't have answers, they prayed for our family. They encouraged us to search the Bible for more answers. Because of their care, concern, and fellowship, our faith solidified. We gradually became the confident, prayerful parents our son needed.

Randy Alcorn recommends a similar training regime in his book *If God Is Good: Faith in the Midst of Suffering and Evil.* He says, "Before difficult times come your way, develop habits of studying God's Word, listening to Christ-centered teaching and music, and reading soul-nourishing literature, both nonfiction and fiction. Daily fill the reservoir from which you can draw when facing difficult times—and helping others face theirs."

On-the-Job Training

Maybe some of you developed those habits before a child with special needs entered your world. Or maybe you're more like I was, in need of on-the-job training—or should we call it in-the-hospital training? If the latter is the case, don't lose hope. Be realistic and expect the training to test your patience and stamina. Expect God to honor your efforts to seek Him. Expect His presence to mature and strengthen you, not overnight, but bit by bit.

Bible Study Care Package

You can create your own Bible study kit if your child's hospital stay is scheduled. But if the situation is an emergency or events unfold too quickly for advance preparations, ask your friends to send you a care package stocked with:

- A small Bible in an easy-to-read translation—*The Message* or English Standard Version
- Pens, pencils, and highlighters
- A small journal
- A portable lapboard
- A copy of *A Different Dream for My Child: Meditations for Parents of Critically or Chronically Ill Children* by Jolene Philo
- A copy of *The Praying Life* by Paul Miller
- A small devotional book like *Our Daily Bread*

God has provided many tools for maturing your faith. You can choose from hundreds of Bible study methods—simple to complicated, short periods of time to long, planned to spontaneous. While you're in the hospital at the mercy of either endless boredom or unexpected change, a short, simple plan is a wise choice. Several easy Bible study tools and prayer helps are listed below. They've been selected with parents like you in mind—distracted moms and dads who only have brief, often interrupted snatches of time to study and pray.

To get started, you need a Bible (the chaplain's office will have one) or a computer with Internet access, and maybe a pencil and paper. Look through the Bible study suggestions below and choose one that looks feasible. Then, give it a try. If it doesn't work, try a different one. Or take elements from several methods and adapt them to meet your situation and needs. Keep trying and training and expecting God to speak and show His control over your child's situation.

1. *Different Dream Parenting* Prayer Guides: Turn to appendix A in the back of the book and select the prayer guide best suited to your present circumstances. Read the daily verse and meditate on it. Then read the accompanying prayer. Or, if you prefer, pray through the verse on your own. If more time is available, turn to the verse in your Bible (or on the Internet) and read the entire chapter. In a journal or notebook, write the date along with thoughts and prayers that come to mind.

2. Ask the hospital chaplain for a monthly devotional guide like *Our Daily Bread* or *The Upper Room*, or access them online. Read one devotion each day. Again, if time allows, read the entire Bible chapter containing the day's verse. Write your thoughts and prayers in a journal.

3. Use *A Different Dream for My Child: Meditations for Parents of Critically or Chronically Ill Children* as a daily devotion.

4. Follow a read-through-the-Bible plan. A quick Google search will yield several from which to choose.

If your Bible study and prayer time feels awkward or unnatural at first, don't be discouraged. Don't think you're doing something wrong. The only wrong thing is giving up and doing nothing.

Recognize God's Training Team

Tell God you expect Him to reveal Himself. Shout to Him at the top of your lungs. Ask Him to draw near to you, to open your eyes to His presence, to calm your spirit, and to encourage your heart. Wait for Him patiently, expectantly.

Then with your eyes wide open, look for Him in the skilled hands of a therapist, the comforting presence of a friend who comes to visit, a coincidental meeting with an acquaintance, a card from relatives, or in a Bible verse that speaks to your heart. Recognize His presence in ordinary people and everyday kindnesses that bring reassurance and hope for one more minute, one more hour, one more day of your child's hospital stay.

Dear Jesus, I want to believe that you are present and in control, but I don't know how to recognize you. Through your Word and prayer, train me to see you in the people caring for my child and in what's happening to our family. May your presence give me hope and courage to pass on to my child.

How has God spoken to me today? What training is He asking me to begin? What do I need to get started? When can I fit study and prayer into these hectic, boring days?

Take Time to Reflect

Resources

Books

- Randy Alcorn, *If God Is Good: Faith in the Midst of Suffering and Evil* (Multnomah, 2009).
- Madeleine L'Engle, *Walking on Water: Reflections on Faith and Art* (North Point Press, 1995).
- Paul Miller, *The Praying Life* (NavPress, 2009).
- Jolene Philo, *A Different Dream for My Child: Meditations for Parents of Critically or Chronically Ill Children* (Discovery House Publishers, 2009).

Bible Study Resources

- *Our Daily Bread* online devotions: www.odb.org
- *The Upper Room* online devotions: http://www.upperroom.org/devotional/
- *New Hope Life Journals* provide a yearly reading plan, Bible study strategies, and a prayer journal in one neat package. You can order the print version at www.lifejournal.cc, or sign up for the free online version at www.lifejournal.me.

Online Versions of the Bible

- www.biblegateway.com
- www.biblestudytools.com
- www.studylight.org

Prayer Guides in Appendix A

- Thirty Prayers of Dependence
- Thirty Prayers for a Hospital Stay
- Thirty Ways to Pray for Your Family
- Thirty Prayers for Educators and Therapists
- Thirty Prayers for Grieving Families
- Thirty Scriptures to Pray for Your Children
- Thirty Ways to Pray for Your Child's Character

Juggling Two Worlds

From Chaos to Calm

9

Calm in the Family

And if one can overpower him who is alone, two
can resist him. A cord of three strands is not quickly
torn apart.

Ecclesiastes 4:12 (NASB)

By the time Ben reached his first birthday, I was
really in grieving mode—mourning the loss of the
baby I thought we were going to have. I'm not sure
Paul, my husband, went through that. He always
had more of a "let's roll with it" attitude.

Sarah, mother of Ben,
who has autism and cerebral palsy

High school sweethearts Pete and Chelsea had been married three years when they discovered that their first child was on the way. When Justus was eighteen months old, Chelsea quit her job to concentrate on his increasing behavioral and developmental needs. Six months later, their pediatrician recommended an evaluation. Justus was three when he was diagnosed with autism. Later doctors diagnosed bipolar disorder and a mild mitochondrial disorder as well. Since then, little sister Noelle was diagnosed with Asperger's syndrome. "When Justus was first diagnosed, it was a real crisis in our marriage. I needed help," Chelsea says.

Family members: Pete, Chelsea, Justus, Noelle, and an autism service dog

By the time Franklin was nine months old, John and Patricia were aware of delays in their son's communication skills. The pediatrician repeatedly brushed aside their concerns at Franklin's checkups. So Patricia, who has a degree in communications disorders, initiated a self-referral. Their little boy was two when diagnosed with autism. Soon afterward their second child was born. "The greatest gift we can give our children," Patricia says, "is a strong marriage."

Family members: John, Patricia, Franklin, and Truman

Wanda knew her unborn child had a 50-50 chance of inheriting branchio-oto-renal (Melnick-Fraser) syndrome, a rare genetic disorder. Her brother was born with it, but her twenty-four nephews and nieces were not. Wanda was a single mom, so her mother accompanied her to the delivery room. When Thomas was born, his grandma immediately recognized the facial features associated with the syndrome. At first, the doctors thought the anomalies were cosmetic. But in the next few months Thomas developed breathing, eating, and hearing issues. After several months of solo parenting, Wanda quit her job. She and her son moved from Texas to California to live with her parents.

Family members: Wanda, Thomas, Grandpa, and Grandma

Paul and Sarah had been married for almost four years when their second child, Ben, was born. During delivery, Sarah's uterus ruptured, and their son was without oxygen for sixteen minutes. Originally given only a two percent chance of survival, Ben beat the odds and lived. Life changed for Paul, Sarah, and their two-year-old Will after Ben's birth. At six months he was diagnosed with cerebral palsy. For years he dealt with terrible eczema. At age twelve he was diagnosed with autism. Sarah says that by the time their two younger sons, David and Sam, were born, she and Paul had adjusted to their new circumstances. Sarah says, "We had a new way of dealing with marriage."

Family members: Paul, Sarah, Will, Ben, David, and Sam

From Chaos to Calm

Families with children come in all shapes and sizes. Two parents or one. Nuclear or extended. Married, separated, divorced, or single. One child, a few, or a houseful. Whatever a family's configuration, the addition of a child with special needs brings profound changes to its dynamics. For a time, the changes in roles and expectations create chaos.

The four families featured above slowly learned to juggle the demands of special needs caregiving with the ordinary demands of life. Their learning curves varied due to the severity of their child's needs, the strength of their support networks, and their responses to the situation. In every case, learning to juggle wasn't easy.

The parents of Justus, Noelle, Franklin, Thomas, and Ben would tell you it was easier to learn to juggle demands when they had examples to follow. So consider the parents in these four chapters your juggling coaches. In the chapters you'll find advice about how to balance the demands of everyday life with caregiving, including how to reduce chaos in your marriage, in the lives of other siblings, at work, and in your Christian walk. In this chapter, the focus is on what parents—married, divorced, separated, or single—can do to create a stable and secure environment for their child.

101

Married with Children

A couple months after our son was born, I was ready to throw in the towel. My breasts were sore from weeks of pumping and my hormones were in overdrive. Sleep deprivation had rubbed my emotions raw. "People have their first child only because they have no idea how hard it is to be a parent," I wailed to my husband. "I can't do this one more day. I just can't."

Hiram listened quietly, then picked up our crying baby. Unperturbed by my outburst, he settled into the recliner with Allen, leaned back, and jiggled our son's diapered bottom. "I'll sleep here with him until he settles down." He smiled. "You go to bed."

I laid down but couldn't sleep. Resentment dogged me. *Why does everything bother me more than it does Hiram?* Guilt invaded my thoughts. *What kind of mother am I, letting my husband sleep in a recliner with our baby instead of doing it myself?*

Then grief engulfed me. *I want to nurse our baby and rock him to sleep instead of pumping milk and pouring it down a feeding tube.*

Finally anxiety took over. *What if he gets sick and has to go to the hospital again? What if he needs more surgery?*

Night after night, we repeated the scenario. Allen fussed. Hiram slept with him in the recliner. I lay in bed, exhausted and sleepless, wondering how my husband could accept our situation without any sign of resentment or disappointment. Why wasn't he as anxious as I was about our baby's condition? Why didn't he talk about his feelings and express more emotion? Decades later, I am amazed that our marriage survived the stresses created by our totally different responses to the guilt, grief, and anxiety inherent in raising a child with special needs.

Differing Responses by Spouses

When one parent's response to a child's special need differs from that of the other parent, stress can build in a marriage. Sarah describes her feelings about her husband's attitude in the early years of caring for Ben: "I felt like Paul didn't appreciate the burden I was carrying. He pretty much shrugged his shoulders and got on with the business of life. Thirteen years later, I can appreciate that personality trait in my husband. It's a good balance to my overly emotional, deep-thinking tendencies."

When Chelsea's second child exhibited developmental differences similar to her son, Chelsea says, "My husband, family, friends, and church family focused on what I was doing wrong as a mom." In desperation, she took a six-day vacation to determine what God wanted her to do. She returned home resolved to do two things: "We needed to get counseling for our marriage, and I needed to be involved in our kids' treatment and therapy."

Patricia reminds us, "We have to realize that spouses have different strengths and weaknesses." At the end of the day, she says, both parents should look back and say, "I did the best I could."

Grief

Often parents of kids with special needs don't recognize grief for what it is. They think, *My child is alive, so what do I have to grieve about?*

John and Patricia's Marriage- and Family-Strengthening Techniques

1. Take turns being in charge. In our house on Saturdays, one parent takes charge while the other gets the day off.
2. Get a sitter once a month.
3. Schedule family time each Sunday.
4. Schedule alone time with each child in the family.

But parents of kids with special needs do grieve. Every parent interviewed for this book talked about grieving the dreams they had for their children. Grief is the natural response to loss, no matter how great or small the loss may be. It's okay to grieve for the healthy child you imagined, the typical family life you expected, and the milestones that will be delayed or not attained.

You need to understand that you and your spouse may not grieve in the same way or on the same schedule. As Patricia says, "Parents approach things differently. They handle grief and loss differently."

Sarah explained her husband's apparent lack of grief this way: "I wanted Paul to hurt with me over the things we could never experience with Ben, and I didn't think he did. But it wasn't that Paul didn't hurt. He just wasn't going to waste time aching over things he couldn't change."

Much more can be said about grief in families living with children with special needs, and the topic will be addressed in greater depth in chapter 19.

Guilt

Many parents of special needs children experience a great deal of guilt. They either think they caused their child's condition or could have prevented it. They feel guilty because they can't fix what's wrong, because they're angry with God, because they resent their spouse's lack of guilt, or because they're envious of more typical families. They may also feel guilty because they resent the demands of caring for their child.

Most likely, these guilty thoughts are unfounded and need to be confronted before they infect you and your marriage. The best way to confront guilty thinking is by telling your spouse how you're feeling. If your spouse isn't available, tell a trusted friend, pastor, or counselor.

Dos and Don'ts for Banishing Guilt

Do   Take a step back and think of what advice you would give a friend in your situation.

Cut yourself some slack.

Accept God's forgiveness.

Humble yourself and ask for help.

Confess and repent when you make a mistake, and then come up with an action plan to prevent future mistakes.

Don't   Be harder on yourself than you would be on your friends.

Expect perfection from yourself or others.

Refuse to accept forgiveness.

Think you can do everything alone.

Refuse to admit your mistakes.

Adapted from *Getting Rid of the Gloom of Guilt* by Barb Dittrich.

Once I worked up the courage to tell Hiram about the guilty thoughts that kept me awake at night, he said, "Jolene, those are lies. You're a good mom." His reassuring words banished my guilty feelings and restored my confidence so I could sleep at night.

Anxiety

Parents of kids with special needs experience more anxiety than parents raising typical kids. Every day brings something new and unexpected as they make decisions they never anticipated, research medical conditions of which they were previously unaware, and advocate for treatment and support services they never imagined existed. If you experience some sleepless nights like I did or are occasionally consumed by worry, your response is perfectly normal—in a special needs kind of way.

When the worry bug strikes, talk to someone you trust, ideally someone who understands the challenges you face. Seek out a parent of a child with similar special needs or a trustworthy online support group specific to your child's condition and share your concerns. The parent or discussion group members can tell you if you're worrying for good reason or not.

What if your anxiety persists long after your child's condition has stabilized? A study conducted by Dr. Richard Shaw and published in 2006 by the Academy of Psychosomatic Medicine found that "parents of kids with special needs often develop anxiety issues." The anxiety can be a symptom of post-traumatic stress disorder (PTSD), which develops when parents experience repeated traumas associated with a child's condition or treatment.

If the anxiety persists more than a few months, the likelihood of developing PTSD increases. If left untreated, both disorders can weaken a marriage and lead to poor parenting. If you suspect that you or your spouse suffers from an anxiety disorder or PTSD, seek assistance from a qualified counselor.

Staying Married with Children

Anxiety and PTSD aren't the only reasons for spouses to seek professional help. As Patricia said earlier, "The greatest gift we can give our children is a strong marriage." If your marriage needs shoring up, get help. Chelsea visited a professional Christian counselor weekly for a year, sometimes alone and sometimes with her husband, Pete. "I discovered some unhealthy relationship habits formed in my childhood and learned to draw boundaries in my roles as an adult daughter, mother, and wife. I learned a great deal and am now able to help other moms."

Paul and Sarah went to their pastor for counseling. "We learned that some of our issues were normal marriage issues. I didn't believe it at the time," Sarah admitted. "Eventually I discovered that all happiness wasn't gone. We had to figure out ways to focus on our marriage because our life was so child-centered during those early years. When Ben got a little older, we established regular date nights, something I wish we'd done much sooner. It was just a new way of doing marriage."

Five Ways to Find a Marriage Counselor

1. Ask a hospital pediatric social worker or chaplain for recommendations.
2. Ask your pastor for recommendations.
3. Call your county or community mental health clinic. Some clinics offer marriage counseling. Be aware that the range and quality of services varies.
4. Call the counselor at your child's school for a recommendation.
5. Use the counselor locator at the Christian Care Network: http://www.aacc.net/resources/find-a-counselor/.

Be sure any counselor you consult is state licensed, certified, and properly credentialed.

If you and your spouse are struggling, seek professional counseling. Call your hospital, mental health clinic, or church for recommendations. Shop around until you find a counselor you and your spouse trust. Do all you can to give your kids the gift of a strong marriage.

Single with Children

If you are a single parent, you and your former partner can give your child the gift of cooperative co-parenting. To do so, you must put your child's needs ahead of your feelings and communicate effectively with your child's other parent. Otherwise, important details will get lost in the shuffle, or your child may manipulate both parents.

If necessary, find a neutral third party to bridge the communication gap. If you can't find a family member or friend to fill the role, perhaps a social worker or pastor can point you to organizations or people who can. Finding the right person may not be easy, but if the end result is effective co-parenting of your child, it's worth it.

Sometimes Mom or Dad has to do the job solo. Being a single parent of a child with special needs isn't easy, but it can be done. Wanda's story is proof of that. Though Wanda parents Thomas by herself, she has a great support system. By moving from Texas to California, she and Thomas could relocate to her parents' home and surround themselves with their large, extended family. "It's good for him to grow up with cousins, aunts, uncles, and grandparents," Wanda says.

If you're the single parent of a child with special needs, you may need to follow her lead and draw on the resources of your extended family. Also, in California, Wanda is able to access financial assistance and programs not available in Texas. She advises being organized and persistent when trying to access state and educational resources. She says, "I am a very squeaky wheel."

Above all, Wanda is realistic about what she can do to meet Thomas's needs. She knows outside help is sometimes required. As a single parent, the best thing you can do for your child is be realistic and seek help when you need it.

A Cord of Three Strands

Whatever the makeup of your family, remember God created it. He created you to be the parent of your child. He created you to ask Him for help as you build a stable, secure family environment. Ecclesiastes 4:12 says, "A cord of three strands is not quickly torn apart" (NASB). Ask God to be the third strand in your family, holding you and your children together in a strong, unbreakable cord.

He's ready. He's waiting. Take God at His word and ask.

Dear Father, the stresses of parenting can be overwhelming. The emotions of guilt, grief, anxiety, and differing expectations are straining my relationships. Show me how to deal with this stress and relieve the burden so I have energy to meet my child's needs.

What do we need to do to strengthen our marriage? Would professional counseling improve our relationship? Where can we find assistance to co-parent effectively? Who can help ease the demands of single parenting?

Take Time to Reflect

Resources

- Christian Care Network: http://www.aacc.net/resources/find-a -counselor
- Snappin' Ministries, a special needs parents' network: www.snappin.org
- To learn more about stress and trauma, see Dr. Richard Shaw, "Acute Stress Disorder Among Parents of Infants in the Neonatal Intensive Care Nursery," *Psychosomatics* 47:206–212, May–June 2006, http://psy.psychiatryonline.org/cgi/content /full/47/3/206; and Laurie Tarkin, "For Parents on NICU, Trauma May Last," *New York Times*, August 24, 2009, http:// www.nytimes.com/2009/08/25/health/25trau.html.

10

Calm with the Sibs and Extended Family

Friends love through all kinds of weather, and families stick together in all kinds of trouble.

Proverbs 17:17

No one will be in the life of a child with special needs longer than a sibling. No one spends more time with them over a lifetime.

Don Meyer, founder of SibShops

More than once, when we were up to our elbows in meeting our firstborn's special medical needs, my husband and I would ask one another, "How do parents with more than one child do this? It would be so hard."

Six years later, after Allen's health issues were mostly resolved, our daughter came along. Perhaps I was a bit smug about how we'd weathered Allen's frequent health crises, by then a thing of the past. Surely his special needs would not impact her life in any significant way.

Fast-forward twenty years, past Allen's unexpected major surgery at age fifteen and his battle with post-traumatic stress disorder (more on that in chapter 22), to the summer after Anne's sophomore year in college. In her quiet, intent manner, she said, "You know, I wasn't even alive when Allen was so sick, but everything he went through changed my life, too."

At first, her statement wounded me. I hadn't been able to protect my son from pain and suffering, but I had hoped to shield my daughter from a world of hurt. Then I stepped back and considered her exact words. She said Allen's experiences had *changed* her life, not that they had *hurt* her.

What Anne said is true. Being the sibling of someone with special needs is life changing. In many cases, those siblings become more compassionate and accepting of others. The special needs of one child do not have to hurt their siblings.

This chapter investigates strategies that help children cope with the life-changing experience of having a sibling with special needs. We'll also talk about supporting extended family members—grandparents, aunts, uncles, cousins—who are impacted by your family's situation.

The Hospital and Sibs

When a child is hospitalized, it affects the whole family. If the hospitalization is unexpected, the experience can be traumatic for brothers and sisters at home. Young kids wonder where their parents or sibling went, or why the new baby they've been anticipating hasn't come home. School-age children may resent the grandparent or babysitter caring for them because they don't follow Dad and Mom's routines and rules. They may worry about "catching" what their sibling has.

Adolescents and teens often have a better understanding of what's happening. They may grieve lost dreams for their sibling or try to relieve their parents' stress by taking on household burdens too heavy for their young shoulders.

The disruption caused by hospitalization can't be avoided, but with good communication, it can be alleviated. Here are some creative methods of communication developed by parents like you.

Mail Call: During her newborn son's ten-day hospital stay, Diana wanted to stay in contact with her two older boys, ages eight and five. They were both in school and the hospital was an hour away, which made visits during the school week difficult. Phone calls were too emotionally taxing for Diana, so she wrote them daily notes. Her husband, Perry, picked up the notes each day when he visited and delivered them to the boys. Then the boys would write notes or make something for Dad to take to Mommy and Sam, their new baby brother.

The notes not only kept the siblings connected to their mom during a stressful time, but they also became treasured keepsakes. Diana put the notes in a box. Every fall, around Sam's birthday, she opens the box and reads the notes, full of misspellings. She looks at the construction paper art projects. Sometimes Sam goes through them, too. "He's intrigued by the story of his hospitalization," Diana says.

Skype and Chance Meetings: After her son's premature birth, Melody was in NICU with Jaxson for 110 days. As often as possible, she Skyped with daughter Reagan, age five, and Kenady, age three, who were at home with their dad, Ryan. "According to NICU policies, they were too young to visit the unit, but we talked almost every day," Melody said. "I would point the camera at Jaxson so they could see their baby brother. Even so, they didn't really get it. I think they thought Jaxson was a doll, not a baby."

Melody shared her concerns with Jaxson's primary care NICU nurse. The nurse came up with a way for the two big sisters to see their baby brother, now two months old. She told Melody when Jaxson would be transported to another department for some tests the next day. "If you and your daughters happen to be waiting in the hall, and they happen to see their baby brother when we walk out of the elevator, there's no hospital policy against that."

Melody describes the meeting: "The nurses had him wrapped up so the girls could unwrap him like a present. Finally they realized their brother wasn't a doll. He was a real, live baby. The nurse used my camera to take pictures and shoot video of our three children together. Then we walked Jaxson to the procedure room and waited till it was over so we could walk back with him. After we got to the lobby of the NICU, the transport team let me have the girls hold their little brother for the first time. That was a wonderful day."

Photographs: Jim and Kathie's fourth child, Tara, was born healthy. She became sick a week later and spent three months in the hospital with Kathie constantly at her side. Two of Tara's siblings, Tori, age three, and Jacob, age two, handled the crisis well. They loved staying with their aunts. But Kathie sensed her oldest son, Elijah, age nine, was struggling with the possibility of Tara dying. She talked to the child life specialist, who arranged counseling for her son. Eventually Jim and Kathie brought him to visit Tara in the hospital. She was at her worst, near death and on a vent, but they wanted him to have a chance to tell her good-bye.

Happily, Tara lived. Unfortunately she's been hospitalized numerous times since her first long stay, though never for as long or for such a critical illness. Each hospitalization worries Elijah, so Kathie takes pictures of Tara with her phone and e-mails them to Elijah to reassure him. "It sounds weird," she says, "but the therapist says to go ahead."

She adds, "Elijah has a framed picture of Tara when she was very sick in his room. When I asked him why, he said, 'Because it reminds be of when our family changed and became better.'"

Picture Books: When Jason and Nancy's son Sam was born, their other two boys were toddlers. The boys were confused because their mom was gone and the new baby didn't come home. They were too young to understand what was happening or to visit the hospital. So for several days, Nancy took digital photos of Sam in NICU and uploaded them at Shutterfly, an online photo printing service where

Ways to Communicate from the Hospital with Sibs

E-mail often
Mail notes and art projects back and forth
Skype with the sibs
Arrange for sibs to visit the hospital
Send photos with your cell phone
Take photos and make a small album
Create a hospital storybook using Shutterfly or Snapfish

customers can create calendars, books, and other products with pictures. She used the photos and a simple narrative to create a picture book of Sam's life.

When it arrived, Jason read the book to Sam's brothers. Nancy says the book helped her little boys understand why Mommy and the new baby weren't at home. Even now, with the entire family together at home, they like to read the story of Sam, their baby brother, in the hospital.

Sibshops and Other Organizations

Of course, not all kids with special needs require hospitalization. Still, the presence of a child with special needs in a home changes family dynamics. The more demanding the care needs and the longer their duration, the more siblings will be affected. Just like parents, they need a support system to help them adjust.

In 1990, Don Meyer created SibShops, a program dedicated to helping sibs adjust to their changed families. Years later, the program reaches kids all over the United States and in several countries. Nancy, who has two children with special needs, says, "My step-kids were SibShop volunteers as teens and my younger children have just started participating. I definitely recommend it." To find the chapter nearest you, visit the SibShop website.

The SibShop website also has many resources for kids. It hosts several Listservs for siblings of differing ages. After registering with the Listserv, kids and adults siblings become part of an online mailing list. Through the list, they can participate in discussions pertinent to their lives. The SibShop online book store has an impressive selection of publications geared for siblings of every age, even adult siblings.

Social workers, child life specialists, or chaplains at the closest university or children's hospital may also conduct sibling workshops or support groups. Two other national programs worthy of note are Big Brothers Big Sisters and Gilda's Clubs. If the siblings of your child with special needs could benefit from the time and attention of an adult mentor, check out Big Brothers Big Sisters at www.bbbs.org. Gilda's Clubs (named for comedienne Gilda Radner who died of ovarian cancer in 1989) supports patients and families dealing with cancer. They offer lectures, workshops, support networks, and activities for adults and children. They have clubhouses in several states and an online community called the Living Room. All their services are free of charge and can be accessed at www.gildasclub.org.

Parents and Sibs

Administering fair and consistent discipline is a challenge for every parent, but the challenges multiply for parents raising both typical kids and kids with special needs. Kids are all about fair, and to them, the differences in your expectations for them and their sibling with special needs may not appear to be fair. Typical siblings may also resent the extra time and attention required to care for your child with special needs, not to mention the disruptions created by appointments, unexpected hospital stays, and behavior meltdowns. See "Dos and Don'ts for Dealing with Siblings" and the resources at the end of this chapter for tips on how to parent children struggling with your family's situation.

Dos and Don'ts for Dealing with Siblings

Don't   Expect siblings to be perfect.

Expect them to behave more maturely than other children their age.

Require them to be their sibling's caregiver.

Ignore signs of their resentment and frustration with their sibling.

Think you can meet all their needs.

Neglect time alone with typical siblings.

Do   Allow siblings to make mistakes.

Hold them to age-appropriate behavior standards.

Give them time with friends and activities separate from the world of special needs.

Allow siblings to honestly express how they feel about their brother or sister with special needs.

Find someone to mentor your typical kids.

Schedule one-on-one time with your typical children.

Still suffering from worry pangs for the siblings? Dealing with some guilt about the way their lives have changed? Seeing signs of stress in them? Sarah, who you met in chapter 9, has some helpful final advice: "Be aware of your other children—observe them when you can. When I sense my boys are stressed, I make time to be alone with them. Sometimes they open up about things that are bothering them. Other times, they're grateful for alone time with Mom or Dad—or a chance to eat out without having to deal with their brother's special needs."

Finally, hear these reassuring words from Julie, a young mom and sister to Jennifer, who has developmental delays. She says, "Give the siblings extra time to adjust. Teach them that it's okay to be different. It can take a long time for them to realize that having a sibling with special needs is a great gift."

Grandparents and Other Extended Family Members

Like you, extended family members are grieving the loss of dreams for their grandchild, niece, nephew, or cousin. If they can't acknowledge or express their grief, they sometimes withdraw or make hurtful comments. Members of older generations may not know how to respond to your child. Until the 1980s many children with special needs were institutionalized, so these adults may need someone to teach them how to interact. Their lack of understanding may also lead to thoughtless remarks about your parenting skills.

When those things happen, do your best to forgive. Assume the best rather than the worst, and try to keep communication lines open. Take every opportunity to explain your child's condition to extended family. Encourage them to be involved in your child's life. If that doesn't work, try not to be bitter or angry. Set boundaries that allow your relationships with them to be as healthy as possible and develop relationships with other people who are more supportive.

Involving Extended Family Members in Your Child's Care

1. Phone or e-mail with frequent updates about your child.
2. Recommend special needs websites.
3. Pass along useful books or articles.
4. Invite them to workshops, conferences, and fundraisers.
5. Invite them to your child's therapy sessions or doctor's appointments.
6. Demonstrate how to connect with your child.
7. Bring a support worker or caretaker to family gatherings.
8. Arrange adult-only outings to nurture your relationships with extended family.

Adapted from *More than a Mom* by Amy Baskin and Heather Fawcett

Beyond Siblings and Extended Family

Thankfully, God's care network extends beyond your family members. Many friends, coworkers, church family, and neighbors are eager to ease the load while you, your kids, and your extended family adjust to this new normal. Let's move on to chapter 11 and learn more about how to accept the gifts they offer.

Dear Creator of our family, I worry about my children. Am I neglecting them? Do they miss me? Surround them with your love when I'm pre-occupied with caregiving. Show me how to make time for them, to express my love to all my kids. Bring caring people to help nurture them and make them feel secure.

What signs of stress are my typical children exhibiting? What resources could help them? How can I find alone time for them and keep communication open? Who can help arrange for counseling? How can we involve extended family in the life of our child with special needs?

Take Time to Reflect

Resources

Books

- Amy Baskin and Heather Fawcett, *More than a Mom: Living a Full and Balanced Life When Your Child Has Special Needs* (Woodbine House, 2006).
- Foster W. Cline and Lisa Greene, *Parenting Children with Health Issues: Essential Tools, Tips, and Tactics for Raising Kids With Chronic Illness, Medical Conditions, and Special Healthcare Needs* (Love and Logic Press, 2007).
- Foster W. Cline and Jim Fay, *Parenting with Love and Logic* (NavPress, 2006).

- Jane Nelsen, Steven Foster, and Arlene Raphael, *Positive Discipline for Children with Special Needs: Raising and Teaching All Children to Become Resilient, Responsible, and Respectful* (Three Rivers Press, 2011).
- Jane Nelsen, *Positive Discipline* (Ballantine Books, 2006).
- Charlotte Thompson, *Grandparenting a Child with Special Needs* (Jessica Kingsley Pub, 2009).

Organizations

- Big Brothers Big Sisters: www.bbbs.org
- Gilda's Club: www.gildasclub.org
- The Sibling Support Project (SibShop): www.siblingsupport.org

Photo Services

- Snapfish: www.snapfish.com
- Shutterfly: www.shutterfly.com

Calm at Work and Home

Yes, we should make the most of what God gives,
both the bounty and the capacity to enjoy it,
accepting what's given and delighting in the work.
It's God's gift!

Ecclesiastes 5:19

Juggling the demands of my kids and my work is
difficult. I don't want to apologize to an employer
for being the kind of parent my children need. So I
have to ask myself, "Will what I'm doing benefit my
kids?".

Chelsea, mother of two kids on the
autism spectrum who have
mitochondrial disorders

The timing of our son's birth was impeccable. His due date
was one week after the last day of school, but all signs pointed to an
early arrival. On Saturday morning, the day after school dismissed,

I tidied my classroom and left a note in case I didn't make it to the official checkout on Monday. Then I went home and watched Hiram plant our garden. Before going to bed that evening, we practiced Lamaze exercises. We were halfway through them when my water broke. Three hours later, Allen entered the world.

I was grateful for his debut a week ahead of schedule. It gave us seven more days together, almost three full months, before the new school year began in August. My gratitude increased after his tracheoesophageal fistula was diagnosed and as his medical adventures continued throughout the summer. By the time the new school year began in late August, his condition had stabilized. I had enough sick days for the steady stream of appointments, procedures, and follow-up surgeries throughout his first year of life.

My husband's work schedule wasn't as flexible as mine. But whenever Hiram asked the ranch's gruff and grumbly business manager if he was out of sick leave or vacation days, the crusty bachelor's answer was always the same: "Last time I checked, you had plenty." Not once did he dock Hiram's pay.

Our support network extended beyond our employers and coworkers. When we were away from home for over a month after Allen's birth, our friends weeded and watered the garden planted the day before our baby was born. When they heard we were coming home, they got rid of moldy leftovers in the refrigerator and restocked it. During Allen's second emergency hospitalization in late July and half of August, they harvested and froze our garden produce. For a year, while we juggled work, family responsibilities, and frequent hospital stays, they cleaned our house, arranged a fund-raiser, and made life bearable. Their hands-on support continued for the next three years, until we moved to another state. Our hearts, and perhaps theirs too, broke when we left that tiny, loving community.

Unfortunately, many work schedules aren't as family-friendly as mine. Many employers aren't as generous as Hiram's. Many communities aren't as supportive or aware as the tiny town where we lived.

Yet your coworkers, neighbors, and friends want to become part of your support system. They just don't know what to do.

This chapter will help you create a functional support network that extends beyond your family. Let's begin with your workplace.

On the Job

Parents of kids with special needs often miss work, and even the most generous employer knows that a workplace can't function efficiently and indefinitely with the absence of a valued employee. It's in both of your interests to find out-of-the-box ways to balance the demands of your child's care and those of your job. The following suggestions and resources may help you.

Employment Leave: Become an expert on your employer's sick leave, professional leave, and vacation policies. Meet with your boss or the person who makes employee leave decisions in your workplace. Explain your situation and ask questions about how to maximize your leave time. Perhaps your employer would allow coworkers to donate leave hours to you. If necessary, you can request family leave as stipulated by the federal Family and Medical Leave Act (FMLA) of 1993. It allows twelve weeks of *unpaid* leave during any twelve month period. More information can be found at the U.S. Office of Personnel Management website (www.opm.gov/oca/leave/html/fmlafac2.asp).

Flexible Job Arrangements: Some jobs lend themselves to flexible work arrangements. Perhaps your employer will let you telecommute, job share, or transfer. The personnel office of a retail chain allowed one dad to transfer to a store near the hospital where his daughter was undergoing lengthy treatment.

Creative Scheduling: By tag teaming, two working spouses can maximize leave time. Sometimes, extra days can be gained by scheduling procedures and surgeries before long holiday weekends or vacations. Hiram and I combined tag teaming with creative scheduling when our son was fifteen. The doctor agreed to schedule a complicated surgery to remove two-thirds of Allen's esophagus a few weeks before Christmas vacation. I was with Allen the first week, and Hiram stayed with him the second week. By then, the school Christmas break had started. I relieved Hiram at the hospital, and he went back to work. Allen was released from the hospital shortly before Christmas, and we made it home in time to open presents. Not the best Christmas vacation, but it was better than docked pay. Also, Allen missed fewer days of school than would have otherwise been the case, which lessened his amount of makeup work.

Military Families: Specialized Training of Military Parents (STOMP) was created to assist military families of individuals with special needs. This federally funded program provides support, training, and information for parents and other family members. STOMP does not arrange leave for military personnel, but can point families to resources. It also helps families access services wherever they are stationed. A complete listing of their services and contact information can be found at www.stompproject.org.

New Employment: Depending on your circumstances, a different job may solve your employment issues. When the parents of a baby girl learned their daughter would never walk or advance beyond the mental ability of an infant, her father changed careers. He left a sales job requiring extensive travel and found one closer to home with regular hours so he could be more involved with her care.

Some parents switch to home-based employment or start a home business. In other cases, one parent leaves the workforce to become the child's primary caregiver.

Before deciding to switch or terminate employment, carefully weigh all considerations, including insurance coverage. Seek professional advice. Talk to a hospital social worker about government financial or health care assistance. Seek legal advice. Meet with a financial planner. Talk to a pastor. Pray with your spouse. Wait to make a final decision until you have explored every possible avenue and are well rested and calm.

Dos and Don'ts for Changing or Terminating Employment

Do   Take time to consider choices

Ask for advice from people you trust

Seek professional advice

Talk and pray with your spouse

Consider what's best for your family's present and future needs

Don't   Make a decision when emotional

Make a decision by yourself

Seek advice of only family and friends

Neglect seeking God's will about the decision

Decide based on only present needs

Around the House

All kids are full of surprises. But kids' special needs add an extra dimension of craziness to parenting. Five minutes after your house is finally calm and under control, a behavioral meltdown or emergency hospitalization can throw everything and everyone into chaos again. In the best of times, ongoing care demands make it hard to get everything done. And the likelihood of downtime—a nap or an hour alone at the coffee shop? Not happening in your lifetime.

But hang on! Who says you have to do everything by yourself? What about those friends, coworkers, neighbors, and people from church who keep asking what they can do? Maybe they can help. But how do you find the energy to tell them what to do when you don't have the energy to clean the sink?

David and Nancy found an answer to that question after their daughter, Hope, was born. Her special needs were extensive and terminal. Many people offered to help, so Nancy referred them to two volunteer coordinators. One coordinated household tasks such as cleaning, laundry, and yard work. The coordinator even trained workers so David and Nancy didn't have to. The other coordinator scheduled meals and made sure the menus were varied.

You can adapt volunteer coordinators for your situation. If you aren't sure what jobs to outsource, see the suggestions below.

- *Yard Work:* Ask for help with snow removal or lawn mowing.
- *Meals:* Have others provide dinners or sack lunches for your typical children.
- *Laundry:* If you're staying at the hospital, arrange for someone to bring you fresh clothes once a week and take soiled laundry home to wash.
- *Transportation:* Have someone assume your car pool duties or arrange rides for you, your kids, your spouse, or others who want to visit the hospital.
- *Housecleaning:* Ask someone to clean the house weekly. If you've been away from home, have someone clean out the refrigerator.
- *Child Care:* Depending on your circumstances, ask family members or close friends to move into your home to care for your healthy children, take your kids to their home, or babysit for a night.
- *Shopping:* Have a power-shopping friend purchase groceries or other things you need.

- *Pet Care:* Have someone feed, water, and exercise your pets.
- *Special Events:* Ask a friend to plan a birthday party and make the cake, or decorate the tree and wrap presents at Christmas.
- *Check the House:* If you're away from home, have someone look for leaky pipes and faucets, reset the thermostat, water plants, and check the lights every day or two.

At the end of the chapter, you'll find information about menu planners and caregiver notebooks designed to make life easier for you and your volunteers.

In the Checkbook

What if you need more than an extra set of hands? What if you need financial support because of lost pay and extra bills? Resources exist to help parents with payments for the mortgage, rent, utilities, child care, and other expenses. Janelle Holst Kamba, a pediatric social worker, says, "These resources are often limited and require a proof of financial need to qualify, but are well worth the effort in applying. A social worker can assist you in identifying and accessing these resources."

The people in your support system care about your financial burden, too. Though it may be hard to disclose your money woes to family, friends, and neighbors, they won't have a clue about your needs unless you say something. The people around you may be willing to organize a fund-raiser, like our friends did way back when. Their efforts will have a threefold effect. Your financial situation will improve, the publicity surrounding the event will teach the public about the disease or condition affecting your child, and the outpouring of love and support will encourage your family.

My husband and I understood those truths when our friends asked if they could do a fund-raiser for us. But it was still hard to say yes and accept their contributions. Hiram and I decided that when we were once again on solid financial ground, we would contribute to fund-raisers for families of kids with special needs whenever we could. It's our own version of the movie *Pay It Forward*, and we find great satisfaction in donating to families. So go ahead and accept help now, while anticipating the day when you can pay it forward.

Public assistance, private assistance, and fund-raisers may ease your burden, but good money management and living within your means is essential. Online classes at Dave Ramsey's Financial Peace University (www.daveramsey.com/fpu/) teach families how to create and stick to a budget. Sticking to a budget may seem impossible in light of hospital bills and unexpected expenses, but it's necessary. We'll discuss finances in greater depth in chapter 13.

Create an Emergency Preparedness Plan

Every family should have an emergency preparedness plan. This is especially true of families with children who are on oxygen or have a vent, or have mobility issues. You can download a free emergency preparedness guide at the New York City Office of Emergency Management (OEM) website: www.nyc.gov/html/oem/html/ready/seniors _guide.shtml. Seattle Children's Hospital has emergency preparedness information at http://cshcn.org. Click on "Planning and Record Keeping," and then click on "Emergency Preparedness for Children with Special Needs."

One More Thing

Once your support network is in place, do one more thing. Make time for yourself. Go for a walk. Take a long bath. Read a book, or your Bible. Take a few minutes each day to learn to breathe again, to quiet your heart. God rested. You should too.

Dear Jesus, forgive me for thinking I can do everything by myself. You delegated authority to your friends, the disciples. Why shouldn't I ask others to help carry this load? Grant me humility to do what is best for my child instead of what salves my pride.

How can I balance the demands of work and family? How can I approach my employer about job concerns? Who, among those who have offered us help, can I trust to schedule and train volunteers? What should I ask them to do?

Take Time to Reflect

Resources

Employment Resources

- For a summary of the Family and Medical Leave Act, visit the U.S. Office of Personnel Management website: www.opm .gov/oca/leave/html/fmlafac2.asp.
- Specialized Training of Military Parents (STOMP): www .stompproject.org

Caregiving Resources

- Melissa Bishop and Karen Berg, *The Caregiver Organizer for My Special Needs Child,* available at http://www.thecaregiver organizer.com.

- Free menu-planning programs that help coordinate meals for friends in times of need include www.caringmeals.com and www.takethemameal.com.

Financial Resources

- Dave Ramsey's Financial Peace University: www.dave ramsey.com/fpu/
- Jill and Mark Savage, *Living with Less So Your Family Has More* (Guideposts, 2010).

Emergency Preparedness Plans

- New York City Office of Emergency Management (OEM): www.nyc.gov/html/oem/html/ready/seniors_guide.shtml
- Seattle Children's Hospital Emergency Preparedness Information: http://cshcn.org

12

Calm at Heart

Turn to me and have mercy on me; grant your
strength to your servant and save the son of your
maidservant.

Psalm 86:16 (NIV)

We are finding ways for Franklin to find God. We do
that by discovering what he loves, and then bringing God into it. That gives us peace.

Patricia, mother of Franklin
who has autism

Sometimes I look back at my first few years of teaching and
shake my head. For some reason, I thought I had to be prepared for
the entire nine months of school before the first student entered the
classroom. So every August, I worked myself into a frenzy reading
textbooks, making worksheet files, scheduling units, and organizing
everything in sight.

My methods worked for a few years, until our little baby boy came along and was hospitalized for almost four weeks after he was born. We were home for about a month before complications sent us back to the hospital. Allen and I arrived home from that stint only a week before school was to begin. No way could I prepare for the entire year in seven short days. Clearly, I needed a new strategy. So I asked myself a few questions: *What's already in place? What must be ready for the first week of school when the kids arrive? What can wait until later?*

The first day of school approached at breakneck speed, and I nearly panicked more than once. But my answers to those questions helped me set right priorities. Much to my surprise, I was well prepared for the first day and even the first week of school.

The lesson learned that fall has served me well ever since. I use similar questions whenever I have a priority-setting session. They can be adapted to my job, housework, family relationships, and relationship with Christ.

No matter how effective your questions are, setting right priorities takes time. It is hard work. So when are you supposed to find time and energy to align your priorities with God's will? And if by some miracle you complete the task, where will you find room in your busy schedule to give your priorities the attention they need?

This chapter helps you answer those questions through a simple, priority-setting exercise and through suggestions about how to keep your priorities front and center. It offers family-friendly strategies for integrating faith and priorities, so you can practice your beliefs and deepen relationships within your family and with God. You may be pleasantly surprised to discover that many of them easy to implement. A few are even downright fun.

Determining God's Priorities

The first step in determining God's priorities for your life is to ask Him to guide your efforts. As you start this process, ask Him to lead you, and then throughout the exercise, when you feel directionless or discouraged or unsure, pray again. Once you've done that, trust His promise in James 1:5: "If you don't know what you're doing, pray to the Father. He loves to help. You'll get his help, and won't be condescended to when you ask for it." Once you've prayed, you can be confident of His promise, whether or not you feel His presence.

In that confidence, spend a few minutes every day this week making a list of your present roles. If you don't know how to begin the list, think about *who you are* instead of *what you do*. If you still aren't sure what to write, the list of my roles may give you some ideas:

- *Faith:* God's daughter
- *Immediate Family:* wife, mother, mother-in-law
- *Extended Family:* daughter, sister, sister-in-law, aunt, niece, cousin
- *Work:* housekeeper, writer, speaker, blogger
- *Church:* Sunday school teacher, discipleship facilitator, women's ministry team member, coffee table baker, small church member
- *Friendships:* close friend, good friend, old friend, mentor, mentee, acquaintance
- *Organizations:* book club member, writers' group member

Once your list is complete, circle the roles you alone can fill. How do you know which ones those are? Well, if the role would cease to exist if you weren't here, then only you can fill it. For example, your personal relationship with God wouldn't exist if you weren't here, so circle it. No one else is your spouse's partner, so circle it. You alone can fill your parental role, make decisions for your aging parent, and share a unique family history with your brothers and sisters. Circle, circle, circle.

How about some of those other roles? You may be the only person able to fill some of them. For example, no one else could write the books I do. But in some cases, someone might be able to take your place. The school system hired a teacher to replace me after I resigned. Your pride may take a beating—we all like to think we're indispensable—but if someone else could fill the role, don't circle it.

Once you're done, look at the circled items. Those are God's top priorities in your life. Those are the roles He created you to fulfill. Those are the nonnegotiables in your life. Most of them, perhaps all of them, are relationships with God and your family. To achieve balance in life, they must be your top priorities.

Fitting in the Other Stuff

Look at the roles that you did not circle. To make all the other stuff fit in, do one of three things: say no, delegate, or seek assistance.

At this stage of life, you must say no to many outside requests. Your conversations will follow this pattern:

"Will you serve on this church committee?"

"No."

"Can you be a Girl Scout leader?"

"No."

"Will you organize a fund drive?"

"No."

Someone else can be on the committee, lead Girl Scouts, or organize a fund drive. Right now, God wants you to concentrate on what you alone can do. Someday your children won't need you as much, and then you can say yes. Until that day arrives, say no often and refuse to feel guilty. Your balancing act is hard enough without a load of guilt weighing you down.

Many of the things you're already doing can be delegated—housework, errands, odd jobs. Perhaps your kids can do some of them. Maybe a relative or close friend will help. Maybe they could become tasks for your volunteer network (see chapter 11). Giving up control may require some serious pride-swallowing and letting go of perfectionism. But oh, the relief when the burden is no longer on your shoulders!

However, some responsibilities can't be delegated to volunteers or resolved with the word no. In those situations, professional services like respite or in-home health care may be a solution. Government assistance may be required to fund priorities associated with your child's care. More information about qualifying for and accessing assistance can be found in chapter 13. For now, we'll continue looking at the priorities you've identified.

Establishing a Right Relationship with God

Once you master the arts of delegating, saying no, and seeking assistance, you can concentrate on what most parents consider their top priorities: faith and family. But first, a word of warning about practicing your faith.

For parents like you, who spend much of the day caring for a child with special needs, it's easy to beat yourself up when you can't find much time to spend alone with God. But you know what? He's not keeping score. He is not in competition with your child. He charged you with the care of your child as surely as He called you into relationship with Him. So you can trust Him to provide ways for you to foster your relationship with Him and with your child.

What are the keys to establishing and maintaining a good relationship with God? Like any relationship, commitment and communication are essential. However, good communication requires time, a commodity in short supply for caregivers. Even if you are committed to your relationship with Christ, how can you find time to communicate with Him? When will you talk to Him through prayer and listen to Him speak through His Word?

The only answer that makes sense for parents immersed in the world of special needs is to talk to Him whenever He provides the chance. You can trust Him to create those opportunities because He's committed to growing a relationship with you. You should be committed to taking advantage of the chances He provides to pray and hear His Word.

Opportunities for Prayer

Paul and Jill Miller are the parents of six children, one of whom has autism. In his book *A Praying Life: Connecting with God in a Distracting World*, Miller describes how he learned to integrate prayer and family. Early on he recognized the moments when he felt most helpless as opportunities for prayer. In fact, he defines prayer as "bringing our helplessness to Jesus" and suggests that whenever we feel helpless, we offer a prayer to God. If you feel as helpless as I did when Allen was a bundle of special needs, that strategy will have you praying all day long!

What might those prayers sound like? According to Miller, your prayer could be one word repeated over and over or a short phrase. You might pray Scripture. Or you might ramble while you search for words to express the longing of your heart.

Whatever words you use, any prayer focused on Christ is pleasing to God. Miller puts it this way, "We look at the inadequacy of our praying and give up, thinking something is wrong with us. God looks at the adequacy of his Son and delights in our sloppy, meandering prayers."

Pray when you feel helpless. Consider those moments of weakness opportunities provided by God to grow your relationship with Him. If you want to pray Scripture, "Thirty Ways to Pray for Your Family" in appendix A is one way to begin. Whatever method you use, whatever your prayer, whatever your need, know that God is waiting to hear you claim the adequacy of His Son.

Opportunities for Reading God's Word

Bruce and Peggy's daughter Lacey is now a young woman, a spastic quadriplegic with the mental ability of a three- or four-month-old child. Her parents are accustomed to her care routine now, but when Lacey was young, Peggy couldn't find enough hours in the day to care for her family and read her Bible.

One day she prayed, "God, you tell your people to read your Word. That is your command. So show me how to follow it."

That same week, Peggy was giving Lacey respiratory therapy to loosen mucus in her daughter's lungs. She was thumping her baby's back when the words "large print Bible" popped into Peggy's mind. Suddenly she realized she could read a large print Bible while administering Lacey's therapy. Peggy says, "Since I had to do the therapy twice a day, I could read for an hour and a half daily."

God showed Peggy a way to regularly read His Word. Her ability to recognize the opportunity came on the heels of prayer. All she had to do was act on it. If you want to follow God's command to read His Word, start where Peggy did. Ask God to show you how to obey Him. Wait for Him to respond creatively. Be prepared to act on the opportunity He provides.

Creative Ways to Spend Time in God's Word

- Listen to an audio Bible while doing housework or driving.
- Read a children's Bible with your kids at bedtime.
- Subscribe to an online daily devotion.
- Memorize Sunday school or AWANA verses with your child.
- Read a large print Bible while doing repetitive tasks.

Fostering Family Relationships

The keys to fostering a good relationship with God—commitment and communication—are also the keys to fostering good family relationships. Just like before, God provides opportunities to strengthen family relationships. These opportunities are waiting in the everyday activities of life—mealtime, chore time, playtime, bedtime. Your job is to be alert to opportunities and turn them into face time with your family.

Ten Face Time Chores

1. Set the table.
2. Fold socks and play laundry basketball.
3. Rake the yard.
4. Bake cookies.
5. Fix supper.
6. Clean a room together.
7. Put on wool socks and "skate" on hardwood floors.
8. Do dishes the old-fashioned way.
9. Ask for help with baby, toddler, or special needs baths.
10. Shovel snow.

Ten Face Time Fun Activities

1. Read books aloud together.
2. Play board or card games.
3. Play Wii bowling or tennis.
4. Have a meeting to plan a special family day.
5. Finger paint or play with clay.
6. Do a jigsaw puzzle.
7. Act out Bible stories or favorite children's books.
8. Have a water fight.
9. Blow bubbles.
10. Go exploring.

How do you start? First, turn off the TV for a half hour every day. While you're at it, turn off the computer, video games, iPods, and anything else that keeps you and your kids from looking one other in the eye. Then use the unplugged time to do things together. Some tasks can be chores, but most should be fun.

By scheduling intentional face time, your kids will see that they are a top priority in your life. God will honor your commitment to connecting with your kids through unexpected blessings, and a renewed sense of delight. When you anticipate being with your kids, you'll feel like our three-year-old son did the first time he scrambled down a roadside ditch to pee in the grass with his dad. Eyes twinkling, he looked up at his father and said, "This is gonna be fun!"

Putting First Things First

Setting right priorities is hard work, but it's work worth doing. When you align your priorities to God's priorities—in your work and in all your relationships—you are truly putting first things first. Once God's first things are in place, the other things will fall into line. Probably not for the next nine months, but for today and maybe this week. This formerly stressed-out school teacher knows that being ready for each day, and maybe for a week, is enough. May it become enough for you, too.

Dear God and Father, a caregiver's life is so stressful. I can't keep balancing all these demands. Show me the roles only I can fill. Give me courage to say no, delegate, and ask for assistance so I have time for what really matters—my relationship with you and my relationships with family members.

What are the things only I can do? When should I say no? What can I delegate? How can I take advantage of opportunities to grow my relationship with you and my family?

Take Time to Reflect

Resources

- "Thirty Ways to Pray for Your Family" in appendix A.
- Paul Miller, *The Praying Life: Connecting with God in a Distracting World* (NavPress, 2009).

Section

4

Long-Term Care Conditions

From Trepidation to Triumph

13

Triumphant at Home

For this reason I say to you, do not be worried about your life, as to what you will eat or what you will drink; nor for your body, as to what you will put on. Is not life more than food, and the body more than clothing? Look at the birds of the air, that they do not sow, nor reap nor gather into barns, and yet your heavenly Father feeds them. Are you not worth much more than they?

Matthew 6:25–26 (NASB)

There's lots of emotion surrounding in-home nursing care. If you previously cared for your child alone or your newborn requires nursing care, as a mom you must guard against feeling inadequate. Guilt can overwhelm you.

Nancy, mother of twins born at twenty-five weeks

Six kids and two parents make Greg and Nancy's house a busy place. Nancy homeschools the three oldest, including twins Phillip and Lillian, who have special needs due to their premature births. Phillip's needs are manageable: asthma, high-functioning autism, and a growth hormone deficiency. But Lillian's are numerous and complex including a seizure disorder, cerebral palsy, and a feeding tube. Her parents were her primary caregivers until the alarming results of a sleep study resulted in the insertion of a tracheostomy (trach) tube. Because of the trach, Lillian was eligible for government-funded in-home care. Nancy says, "Lillian now gets much better care because the nurse focuses exclusively on her."

Care placement: Lillian lives at home and receives in-home care.

At birth, Brant and Melissa's daughter appeared to be a typical newborn, though little Ginny had trouble breast feeding. Over the next few weeks, her poor muscle tone became more noticeable. She wasn't growing. Doctors discovered her hearing loss when she was one. Finally, when she was two, doctors diagnosed Ginny with a rare genetic metabolic disorder. After receiving the diagnosis, Melissa approached a neighborhood church that ran a well-respected preschool about starting a class for kids with special needs. "I'd be willing to help," she said.

Care placement: Ginny lives at home with her parents and attends the church's Department of Human Services (DHS) accredited private preschool for children with special needs.

Joe weighed four pounds, three ounces at birth. LeAndre brought her firstborn home after only a week in NICU. He was six months old when the babysitter expressed concern about his development. Three months later he was diagnosed with cerebral palsy. Later autism was added to the diagnosis. When Joe was little, LeAndre consulted doctors and followed up on every available therapy. She became Joe's sole advocate when her marriage ended. "I demanded horse, speech, pool, occupational, and physical therapy. I would not accept no for an answer. Because of those early therapies, Joe can walk and talk."

Care placement: Joe lives at home with his service dog and returned to public school after being homeschooled for a year when he was fourteen.

Ashley was born after a full-term, normal pregnancy. By the time she'd been home two months, her parents, Reynolds and Kori, were experts at dodging her projectile vomit. At nine months, she received a feeding tube. At thirteen months, she had brain surgery. At five, she was diagnosed with autism. As she grew older, she acted out more and more frequently. Eventually her behavior required inpatient treatment in a psychiatric unit. "She was in a room with padded walls," Reynolds says. "We saw her once a day for thirty minutes. We didn't know what to do." Finally, for the well-being of their daughter and the safety of her younger brother, Ashley's parents placed her in a highly respected residential center for children with special needs.

Care placement: Ashley lives at a residential center and attends public school. Her parents attend her extracurricular activities, and she comes home some weekends.

From Trepidation to Triumph

A staggering array of services exists for kids with special needs. First there's federal government assistance—Social Security and Medicaid. Then there's state funding—income assistance, supplemental insurance, food assistance, and medical supply programs. Nonprofit and private organizations like Easter Seals, Variety Clubs, and the Children's Miracle Network also offer funding and programs. Schools provide services too—early intervention, special needs preschool, and differentiated educational programming.

But that's not all. Other monies and services are available for kids, too. More than parents can keep straight. More than one book can list. So instead of creating lists, the next four chapters outline strategies for locating services that match your child's long-term needs.

This chapter concentrates on government funding and services for children at different levels of care. The second chapter focuses on educational services, while the third explores church and community offerings. The final chapter encourages parents to trust God's timing and provision, conquer discouragement, and overcome guilt while meeting their children's long-term care needs.

A Disclaimer

In the interest of full disclosure, I must confess my lack of expertise concerning long-term care for kids. By the time our son started kindergarten, his early medical needs were resolved, and he no longer required specialized care.

Even so, I'm no stranger to long-term care. My parents were twenty-nine with three children under the age of five when the doctor diagnosed my dad with multiple sclerosis (MS). Soon he was in a wheelchair, able to stay home by himself but unable to work. We cared for him at home as his health declined. Eventually a nurse's assistant came during the day. After twenty-four years of in-home care, Mom made the difficult decision to move Dad into a nursing home where he spent the last fourteen years of his life.

Because of Dad, I know how relentless the demands of daily care can be. I know how invasive the presence of a professional caregiver in the home can feel. And I know how heart-wrenching it is to place a dearly loved family member in residential care.

Still, differences exist between care services for children and adults. Therefore many of the strategies and suggestions in this chapter come from parents and professionals who care for children with long-term needs.

Public Funding and Services

Many children with special needs are eligible for federal programs like Social Security Income (SSI). When asked about government programs for kids, parents say the biggest hurdle isn't a lack of programs, but finding out about and qualifying for programs. They overcome those hurdles by using a combination of strategies.

- Enlist the expertise of the social worker while your child is hospitalized. Social workers know what programs are available and how to fill out application forms.
- If a child's diagnosis didn't require a hospital stay, ask your doctor for information about services. If the doctor can't help, set up an appointment at the nearest Department of Human Services (DHS).
- Whether or not your child has been hospitalized, contact the continuity of care departments at your state's children's and university hospitals. Ask—beg if you have to—for a list of programs and resources.
- If your child is under three years of age, call the public school and ask to be directed to the nearest Early Intervention Service headquarters.
- Talk to parents with children who already receive government monies. Ask for tips about where and how to apply. Or find an online support group and post your questions there.
- If you apply for assistance or services and are denied, don't give up. Call the hospital or school to find a social worker, and ask him or her to help you reapply. If you're denied again, hire a reputable lawyer and apply once more.
- Visit the ARC website at www.thearc.org. ARC is a national group that advocates on behalf of people with intellectual and developmental disabilities. At the website, you'll find clear

and concise information about government programs like SSI, Medicare, Medicaid, medical waivers, and more.

If the idea of accepting assistance from the government doesn't sit well with you, consider Sarah's words: "I know some Christian families are vehemently opposed to taking government funds. But I would rather focus my energies on helping my child than have to go back to work or worry about the bills his very existence creates."

Or maybe you're embarrassed about applying for government assistance. Reynolds and Kori were, too. But as Reynolds explained, "We had to apply, even though I make a good living. Our insurance was maxed out and medical bills were piling up. My dad told me to look at it as a taxpayer. We're getting back what we put in."

Nonprofit and Private Funding

Just as with government programs, the biggest hurdles of nonprofit and private assistance programs are finding and qualifying for them.

- Check the information packet you received while in the hospital. It may list private and nonprofit organizations. If your phone call to a continuity of care department resulted in a resource listing, look through it carefully.
- Go to national and state websites of organizations that support a wide array of special needs (think Easter Seals, March of Dimes, and the ARC). Locate your local chapter and call them to inquire about services. Easter Seals loaned Dad the bed-to-chair lift device and hospital bed he used for two decades.
- If a national foundation exists for your child's condition, search their website for loan programs, scholarships, grants, and other forms of assistance.
- Again, ask other parents, in person and online, what private funding sources they access.
- Contact local service organizations such as Kiwanas, Rotary, Jaycees, the Elks, or Lions Clubs. If the local chapter doesn't

have funds or programs, members may be able to put you in contact with regional or national groups that do.

Five Government Programs to Investigate

- Social Security's Supplemental Security Income (SSI): A federal program designed to help the aged, blind, and disabled who have little or no income. It provides cash for basic needs like food, clothing, and shelter.
- Medicaid: Medicaid is the federal government's health insurance program for low-income persons with disabilities or medical conditions that require considerable assistance.
- Medicaid Waiver Programs: This program "waives" the parents' income and considers only a child's income (no more than $2,000 per year) so children are eligible for Medicaid programs that pay for home health aides, respite care, day care, and more.
- Medically Needy Programs: Some states base eligibility on family income minus medical expenses.
- State Children's Health Insurance Programs (CHIP): If you don't have health insurance and have too much income for Medicaid, your child may qualify for this state program, which is partially funded with Medicaid dollars.

For more information about government assistance programs, contact the nearest Department of Human Services (DHP) office or U.S. Social Security Administration Office.

Adapted from *More than a Mom* by Heather Fawcett and Amy Baskin.

Nancy says, "If you don't get all the services you hoped for, be careful about how you complain. If you're getting something instead of nothing, be grateful."

Optimal Level of Care

Unfortunately there are no standard formulas for figuring out the optimal level of care for your children. However, a pattern emerged as families shared how they determined the right level of care. Most parents provided total care at first (which was all some children ever needed). But in other families, tiny babies grew into adolescents too big to carry. Harmful behaviors escalated. Medical conditions deteriorated, and children became medically fragile. At some point, these parents acknowledged their inability to provide the level of care necessary. When that happened, they sought outside assistance.

For some parents, an occasional respite weekend was enough. For others, a few hours of in-home care every day eased the burden. Some medically fragile children required around-the-clock care. In a few cases, a residential facility was the best option.

Residential facilities are year-round homes for children who need twenty-four hour, professional care. Some residential facilities specialize in a specific category of care: medically fragile children, children with intellectual disabilities, or children who are mentally ill. Others serve a broad range of children with significant care needs.

Finding In-Home Help

A hospital or social worker gives parents of children qualified for in-home care a list of recommended providers, but parents make the final choice. Nancy says, "Even if the social worker takes care of everything, parents should interview more than one agency. They should have a list of questions ready." See appendix D for Nancy's interview questions.

Bev Miller is the director of social services at a children's residential facility in Storm Lake, Iowa. For twenty-three years, she has counseled parents considering residential placement for children between the ages of five and twenty-one. Miller says, "Taking the step to residential care is hard, but by the time parents call with questions, they've already accepted the fact that it's necessary."

Miller recommends parents and families tour the facilities they are considering. During the tour, they should note the building's condition. Is it clean? Neat? How does it smell? Look at the bedrooms and bathroom facilities.

Parents should meet with all team members to tell them about their child. They should ask the following questions:

- Can we make unannounced visits at all times?
- What is the staff-to-client ratio?
- How long has your leadership worked here?
- On average, how long do staff members stay?
- What programs can kids participate in?
- What emergency medical services are in place?
- How are physical and behavioral outbursts handled?
- What are the documentation and communication procedures?
- How involved can parents be?
- How often can we arrange home visits?

Once parents place a child in residential care, Miller says they can expect an adjustment period for themselves as well as for their child. "The hardest thing for parents is giving up day-to-day control of what happens in their child's life. That's the source of the guilt they feel."

Reynolds and Kori know all about guilt. They experienced it when Ashley entered a residential facility. "We didn't want to place her," Reynolds says. "The first two weeks she was gone were as close to death as anything I've experienced. But she couldn't stay at home. Her needs were so great that Kori couldn't function."

Kori adds, "Caring for her was so wearing. I can't tell you how wearing. I finally realized that for us to protect her, we had to let others take over her daily care."

God's Assistance

God called Reynolds and Kori to protect their child, and He provided others to care for her. He calls you to find the best way to care for and protect your child, too. In His complex and mysterious wisdom, He has provided services and funding to assist you. So push through your trepidation and guilt. Advocate for the services your child needs until you obtain them. Doing so is one way you can protect your God-given, beloved child.

Dear God of triumph, I am not adequate for this task. Please show our family how to best care for our child. Lead us to the resources that will allow us to meet every need. Help us to provide the best life possible for our child.

How well are we meeting our child's care needs? What support do we need to give our child the optimal level of care? What is the next step I need to take to access that support?

Take Time to Reflect

Resources

Government Resources

- To browse through the U.S. Department of Health and Human Services listing of state Medicaid waiver programs, visit https://www.cms.gov/MedicaidStWaivProgDemoPGI/MWDL/list.asp.
- To locate the nearest DHS office, type "Department of Human Services" along with your county and state into a search engine.
- To locate the nearest U.S. Social Security Administration office, visit https://secure.ssa.gov/apps6z/FOLO/fo001.jsp.

Nonprofit and Private Resources

- ARC: www.thearc.org
- Chapel Hill Training–Outreach Project (CHTOP), a state-by-state respite care search: http://chtop.org/Search-For-Respite.html
- Disabled Children's Relief Fund: www.dcrf.com
- Easter Seals: www.easterseals.com
- First Hand Foundation: https://applications.cerner.com/firsthand/
- Friends of Disabled Adults and Children (FODAC): www.fodac.org
- Kiddos Clubhouse Foundation: www.kiddosclubhousefoundation.org
- March of Dimes: www.marchofdimes.com
- United Health Care Children's Foundation: www.uhccf.org
- Small Steps in Speech: www.smallstepsinspeech.org

14

Triumphant at School

You're blessed when you can show people how to
cooperate instead of compete or fight. That's when
you discover who you really are, and your place in
God's family.

Matthew 5:9

Look for school professionals who say, "You know
your child best." Those are the ones you want to
work with.

Sharon, mother of Tim,
who has cerebral palsy

Do you remember my disclaimer in the last chapter? The one
about my long-term care experience being with a parent rather than
a child? Well, a similar disclaimer is in order for this chapter. Here
goes.

I have never advocated in the public school special education
arena as a parent. But as a teacher, I advocated frequently for many

students. Some years, a third of the students in my general education classroom had an individualized educational plan (IEP) or their parents and I were in the process of obtaining one. Customizing classroom instruction to meet students' educational needs was my passion. Partnering with parents to help kids achieve maximum success was deeply satisfying. For me, this chapter is an opportunity to partner with you. In our partnership, we'll explore the laws that impact special education and how to advocate so your child will benefit from them.

Alphabet Soup

The language accompanying special education services creates a veritable alphabet soup. Here's a quick overview of what the laws mandate and the abbreviations that refer to the laws.

Individuals with Disabilities Education Act (IDEA): IDEA became law in 1974. The law has been revised several times, most recently in 2004. According to its website, IDEA "is a law ensuring services to children with disabilities throughout the nation. IDEA governs how states and public agencies provide early intervention, special education and related services to more than 6.5 million eligible infants, toddlers, children and youth with disabilities" (http://idea.ed.gov).

IDEA Part B: Children and youth with disabilities (ages 3 to 21) are granted access to special education and other services in this part of the law.

IDEA Part C: This section of the law mandates early intervention services for infants and toddlers with disabilities (birth to age 2). Why didn't the government assign the letters in a logical progression, so infants and toddlers were Part B and older children were Part C? I have no idea!

Early Childhood Intervention: Each state has a different name for the organization or organizations providing early intervention services. The National Early Childhood Technical Assistance Center (NEC-TAC) maintains a directory of each state's early childhood intervention director at www.nectac.org/contact/ptccoord.asp. If you can't find what you're looking for at the site, try googling "early childhood intervention" and your state's name.

Individualized Educational Plan (IEP): IDEA requires an IEP for each student who qualifies for special education services. The IEP documents the results of tests and other measures used to assess a child's level of performance. It lists goals and objectives designed to remediate a child's specific educational concerns and tracks a child's progress in regard to the goals. The IEP goals focus on remediating significant learning problems through instruction, not through medical treatment or physical accommodation.

504 Plans: 504 plans describe the environmental accommodations a school will make so a child's physical disability won't hinder his or her education. Students with 504 plans may need no extra learning assistance, just simple accommodations to remove physical barriers. Students may need extra room for a wheelchair, insulin shots, an amplification system, or help with a colostomy bag.

For clear and easy-to-understand explanations of IDEA, IEPs, and more, visit Understanding Special Education at www.understanding specialeducation.com. For more information about educational law and parent advocacy, visit Wrightslaw at www.wrightslaw.com.

The IEP Team

Remember those hospital care teams you learned about in chapter 6? Well, the IEP team is the educational equivalent. Just as parents are members of a child's hospital care team, they are part of the child's IEP team too. The team includes the principal, special education teacher, school psychologist, and school counselor. Other faculty and staff members, like a classroom teacher (if the child spends part of the day in a general education setting), a school social worker, therapists, and a school nurse, might be on the team as well, depending on the child's needs.

For children ages three and up, IEP meetings begin when testing reveals a need for services. (Note that schools cannot assess students without parental consent.) By law, parents are to be informed of and invited to participate in all IEP meetings, starting with the initial placement and continuing with annual reviews.

Some parents find the meetings uncomfortable. Sitting around a table with all those educators can be intimidating. But as the world's expert on your child (remember, that's you), you should not feel intimidated. You should feel like a valuable team member, someone who has much to contribute to the creation and updating of the IEP.

One effective way to participate is by fostering cooperation and respect among team members. To both show and gain respect, try these parent-tested tips at IEP meetings.

1. Be organized. Keep IEP paperwork in a three-ring binder. Bring the binder to IEP meetings and parent-teacher conferences.
2. Have both parents attend IEP meetings if possible.
3. Ask questions when you don't understand. Keep asking until you do understand.
4. Give school professionals a well-rounded understanding of your child. Give them a glimpse of your child beyond the diagnosis. Help them see your child's strengths. Let them know what your child is feeling. Show them the whole child.
5. Be firm and calm. If you can't stay calm, ask for the meeting to be rescheduled.
6. Watch how you phrase your requests. Instead of demanding to have your ideas implemented, ask for a trial run to see how they work.
7. Make a suggestion, and if no one responds favorably, wait for another meeting to suggest it again.
8. Know which members of the team are receptive to new ideas and talk to them before the meeting about how to present your thoughts. Sit beside them during meetings.
9. Be proactive about who is on your child's team. If a teacher or paraprofessional clicks with your child, see if they can deliver services and thus be part of the team.

10. Be realistic about goals and what you ask teachers to do. If your child needs more attention than the teacher can provide in the present educational setting, advocate for more support and/or services.

These tips should help your team create the best possible educational plan for your child.

Julie, a speech therapist who attends many IEP meetings and is sister to Jenny who has special needs, adds these suggestions for parents.

- Read through the information given at IEP meetings.
- Be aware of whether or not IEP goals are being met at school.
- Teach your child to self-advocate in middle and high school.
- Join a parent support group.
- Research educational options and seek realistic goals.

Remember, if you are not satisfied with the IEP, you do not have to sign it. Instead, ask for another meeting to discuss your concerns. For more information about what to do if you absolutely cannot reach an agreement, visit www.wrightslaw.org or call your state's Department of Education.

The annual IEP meeting is an important component of your child's education, but it's not the only one. Equally important are the relationships you develop with your child's teachers and other professionals. Some parents and educators have perfected the art of cultivating good relationships. Patricia's son Franklin has autism, which makes communication difficult for him. Patricia speaks for her son by:

- Creating a portfolio of Franklin's art creations and writing samples, along with videos of him at play. She takes the portfolio to his IEP meetings so educators can see what her son can do.

- Putting a note about their family's weekend activities in Franklin's backpack on Mondays. His teacher uses the note to initiate conversations with him.
- Creating a simple parent/teacher communication form each fall.
- Using e-mail to coordinate services provided by the professionals on Franklin's IEP team.

Another parent, Cassandra, creates an *All about Me* book featuring her son Caleb for teachers each fall. She includes pictures, information about Caleb's condition, his likes and dislikes, and emergency contacts. She gives the book to teachers before school starts. Forms for Cassandra's *All about Me* book are available for download. See the resources at the end of this chapter.

Dos and Don'ts

Do	Ask for the teacher's opinion
	Focus on positives in teacher and child
	Empower teachers by providing information
	Say thank you
Don't	Order teachers around
	Dwell on the negatives
	Withhold information the teacher needs
	Be ungrateful

Transition to Adulthood

An IEP follows a child until there's no longer a need for services, the child graduates at age eighteen, or the child reaches age twenty-one. By age sixteen, transition services must be addressed in the IEP. These services range from independent living to residential care options, from job training to college to community involvement. These topics will be addressed more completely in chapter 21. If the school doesn't mention transition services during the annual review when your child turns sixteen, be sure you do.

Back to School

When you advocate in the school system, you'll receive an education along with your child. You'll meet teachers who care passionately about kids and try to meet a myriad of student needs with limited time and resources. Because their jobs are so important, as well as stressful and demanding, they need parents to pray for them daily. The prayer guide "Thirty Prayers for Educators and Therapists" in appendix A contains thirty Scriptures to pray on behalf of school personnel. What a powerful way to give spiritual support to the people involved in your child's education!

Dear Jesus, you are the great teacher. Thank you for the laws that insure appropriate education for children with special needs. Lead us to teachers and educators who will value my child. Fill me with your compassion, confidence, and honesty so I can foster good relationships with them.

In what ways is the school meeting my child's needs? Where is there room for improvement? How can I respectfully advocate for needed changes?

Take Time to Reflect

Resources

General Education Resources

- To find your state's Department of Education website, google "Department of Education" along with the name of your state.

Special Education Resources

- The National Early Childhood Technical Assistance Center (NECTAC) directory of Early Childhood Intervention state directors: www.nectac.org/contact/ptccoord.asp
- Wrightslaw: www.wrightslaw.com
- IDEA Department of Education website: http://idea.ed.gov/
- Understanding Special Education: www.understandingspecial education.com
- The Council for Exceptional Children: www.cec.sped.org
- Forms for Cassandra's All about Me book can be downloaded at www.DifferentDream.com. Type "Cassandra" in the search box.
- "Thirty Prayers for Educators and Therapists" in appendix A.

15

Triumphant in the Community

Jesus then said, "I came into the world to bring
everything into the clear light of day, making all
the distinctions clear, so that those who have never
seen will see, and those who have made a great
pretense of seeing will be exposed as blind."

John 9:39

After Nichole was born, I made it my career to know
everything about Down syndrome and my daughter
so I could educate those around me.

Ellen, mother of Nichole,
who has Down syndrome

Being active in the community wasn't easy for my dad once he was restricted to wheelchair. In the 1960s, sidewalks curbs confined him to one city block. Stairs barred him from many public buildings. Narrow front doors and steps kept him from accepting dinner invitations in friends' homes. Lack of access to bathroom facilities made long jaunts from home risky.

But with Mom as his coconspirator, Dad and his wheelchair remained a fixture in our small town for over a decade. Whatever the occasion—ball games, the county fair, church, school events, visits with relatives, or a drive in the country to check crops—Mom lifted him into the passenger seat of the car, and then hefted his wheelchair into the trunk. While Dad discreetly tucked his urinal beneath his feet, my sister, brother, and I scrambled into the backseat, fighting over who had to sit in the middle. Off we went, Mom and Dad scheming a way through the waiting obstacle course.

The older I got, the more embarrassing these forays became. The way people stared at Dad in his wheelchair was bad enough, but he drew attention to himself by constantly waving to friends and strangers, wheeling his chair up to city bigwigs and interrupting their conversations, and hollering at people across the street.

Worst of all were high school and college football games. Once the ticket takers waved Mom through the gate, Dad always stuck his head out the car window and yelled, "Paraplegic! Get out of the way! There's a paraplegic coming through!" The crowds parted like the Red Sea. Mom drove to the edge of the field and parked, while Dad waved to the crowd like a conquering hero.

I, on the other hand, crouched in the backseat and died a thousand deaths, all the while thinking, *Why does my dad have to be so different? Why can't he be like everybody else?*

The answer came many years later at a high school class reunion. A former classmate greeted me and smiled. "You know, Jolene, I remember your dad. He was a really cool guy, the first person in a wheelchair I ever met."

Those words put Dad in a new light. He wasn't Ward Cleaver with a perfect life and family. He and Mom were reality television thirty years ahead of schedule, true survivors and living examples. Their involvement in our community made a difference in the perceptions of a new generation. Not only that, being out and about enhanced Dad's quality of life. And though at the time my siblings and I were too busy fighting in the backseat to notice, our parents' active involvement shaped our lives for the better, also.

But as you know, getting around with a child who has special needs isn't easy. Sure, your evening would be easier if you watched a DVD at home instead of loading your child and a trunk full of equipment into the car and going to the movies. Yes, the hassle of going out to eat with a wild child makes cooking supper at home attractive. And certainly, care demands limit how active you can be. But community involvement is a powerful way for your family to advocate. The more visible you are, the more people learn about your child's condition. As this chapter shows, there are simple ways to be active around town.

Be Visible in Your Community

Thanks to the Americans with Disabilities Act, public facilities are now accessible to those with special needs. Therefore, your family can participate in more community activities than ever before. Here are ten simple ways for your family to be visible around town.

1. Go to the movies. Some theaters offer "sensory friendly" film showings geared for children with autism and other special needs. Visit http://www.amctheatres.com/SFF for more information.
2. Walk dogs or pet animals at the Humane Society.
3. Attend school and community sporting events.
4. Attend children's theater productions and concerts.
5. Walk to the park and play.
6. Go out to eat at a family-friendly restaurant.
7. Check out books at the library. Attend story or craft time, too.
8. Go shopping.
9. Visit the science center, children's museum, or art museum.

10. Play board games with nursing home residents.

Hopefully, those ten ideas will get your community involvement juices flowing. Now, how about challenging your family to come up with ten more things to do in the town where you live?

Be Active in Community Programs

Some national organizations provide programs at the community level for children with special needs. The best known program is Special Olympics, which began in Eunice Kennedy Shriver's backyard in 1962. Now Special Olympics provides opportunities for people with disabilities to participate in sporting events around the country. Another national program, Challenger Little League, was created in 1998 to help children with developmental delays and physical disabilities enjoy baseball. And since its inception, Boy Scouts have welcomed kids with disabilities. They devote an entire website to scouts with special needs.

Where to Learn about Community Programs

Chamber of Commerce
YMCA
Library
Hospital
Public school or your child's
   teachers
Other parents

Local communities have programs too. Once again the problem isn't a lack of programming, but difficulty accessing the programs that exist. To find what's available in your area, some digging may be required. The sidebar can help you begin.

If your local search leaves you empty-handed, try typing "adaptive sports" or "adaptive sports programs" into a search engine. My online search yielded an array of adaptive sports programs across the country: ice skating, buddy basketball leagues, therapeutic horseback riding, and more. If you can't find a local club or chapter for the programs you unearth, contact the regional or national headquarters for assistance.

If your efforts still don't yield results, two options remain. Either give up or advocate for the creation of a new program. Time constraints and responsibilities may force you to do the first. But if you have the resources and the will to pursue the matter, Melissa's story may give you ideas about how to proceed.

Be Part of the Solution

Melissa's young daughter has a rare genetic metabolic disorder. Because of it, Ginny has poor muscle tone, hearing loss, and vision issues. From birth to age three, Ginny received in-home early childhood services. At age three, the services would be delivered through the public school's special needs preschool.

Melissa didn't want to subject Ginny to long bus rides before age six. So she searched for special needs preschools in her area. She found only one. Ginny was eighteen months old when she became child number 150 on the preschool's waiting list. Doubtful that her daughter would reach the top of the list by age three, Melissa explored other options.

She knew of a church in the neighborhood that offered respite care for families of kids with special needs. The church also ran a preschool with a good reputation. "Though we weren't members there, I e-mailed the coordinator in June. I told her I was a former teacher and would help start a special needs preschool if they were interested," Melissa said. "They were interested."

She and the coordinator toured other facilities in the state before designing their own program. Melissa explains, "Because this would be one class in a preexisting program, accreditation and Department of Human Services approval was much easier. The church's support has been outstanding. Members have given grants so children who can't afford the tuition can still attend."

By the start of the new school year three months later, nine students, including Melissa's daughter, entered preschool.

Does Melissa's story inspire you to meet a need in your community? Maybe you could become the leader of a Girl Scout troop that welcomes kids with special needs. Perhaps you can talk to a service club about sponsoring a buddy basketball league, or find a Boy Scout interested in creating a Challenger Little League team for his Eagle Scout project. Or maybe you could raise awareness about the need for a special needs ministry at your church.

Be an Advocate for Special Needs Ministries

In recent years, some church congregations have welcomed families in the special needs community by offering respite programs, training Sunday school teachers, and educating their members about special needs. This inclusion is long overdue.

If your church doesn't have a special needs ministry, consider broaching the subject with church leaders and pointing them to the resources on the following page.

Ephesians 6:4 commands parents to bring up their children in the instruction of the Lord. That's a hard command to obey if your church isn't interested in a special needs ministry, and lack of accessibility and accommodation keeps your family from attending church. You may need to look for a body of believers that welcomes people with special needs and can help you fulfill God's command for parents.

Be at Peace with Your Role

Your roles in the community and at church may be different from those of other parents. They may coach typical kids, while you advocate for the creation of a special needs sports team. Your role may be spearheading a special needs ministry at church or planning a weekly family outing. It could be staying home with a child whose care fully occupies each day.

Special Needs Resources for Churches

- Key Ministry: Founded by Dr. Stephen Grcevich, Key Ministry helps churches meet the needs of every child by providing free resources, training, and several informative blogs. (www.keyministry.org)
- McLean Bible Church's Accessibility Summit: McLean Bible Church, located outside Washington, DC, hosts an annual national summit every April. Church leaders, families, and volunteers can attend workshops on a variety of topics. (www.accessibilitysummit.org)
- Joni and Friends: Through their Christian Institute on Disability, Joni and Friends trains church leaders to start special needs ministries. (www.joniandfriends.org)
- Friendship Ministries: This ministry offers churches curriculum designed for children and adults with intellectual disabilities. Their products are widely used and respected across denominational lines. (www.friendship.org)
- Inclusive Church: At her blog, Amy Fenton Lee addresses current issues and features resources of interest to leaders in churches with special needs ministries. (www.theinclusivechurch.com)
- Disabled Christianity: Dr. Jeff McNair, professor of special education at California Baptist University, writes convicting blog posts about special needs and the church. (www.disabledchristianity.com)
- *Same Lake, Different Boat: Coming Alongside People Touched by Disability*: This book by Stephanie Hubach is a must-read for churches establishing special needs ministries. She writes from the perspective of a church ministry leader and mother of a child with Down syndrome.

Whatever your role, try to be at peace with it. However, if you're like most parents of kids with special needs, you'll feel a little guilty. Or maybe a lot guilty. If so, get ready for chapter 16, which tackles the subject of guilt head-on.

God of strength, so often it is easier to hole up at home than to take my child out in the community. Grant me discernment to know when to rest at home and when to be visible in public. Give me strength for what you want me to do each day.

How can our family be visible in the community? What community programs would benefit my child? What gaps in special needs opportunities exist in this town? How could I advocate to meet them?

Take Time to Reflect

Resources

Community Resources

- Boy Scouts: www.wwswd.org
- Challenger Little League: www.littleleague.org/learn/about/divisions/challenger.htm
- North American Riding for the Handicapped Association: www.narha.org
- Sensory friendly movies: http://www.amctheatres.com/SFF
- Special Olympics: www.specialolympics.org

Church Resources

- Disabled Christianity: www.disabledchristianity.com
- Friendship Ministries: www.friendship.org
- Inclusive Church: www.theinclusivechurch.com
- Joni and Friends: www.joniandfriends.org
- Key Ministries: www.keyministry.org
- McLean Bible Church's Accessibility Summit: www.accessibilitysummit.org
- Stephanie Hubach, *Same Lake, Different Boat: Coming Alongside People Touched by Disability* (P & R Publishing, 2006).

16

Triumphant Faith

His disciples asked, "Rabbi, who sinned: this man or
his parents, causing him to be born blind?" Jesus
said, "You're asking the wrong question. You're looking for someone to blame. There is no such cause-
effect here. Look instead for what God can do."

John 9.2–3

I can say, "This was a mistake." Or I can say, "God
intended Nichole to be this way for a reason." I can
talk about crushed dreams and hold them against
God. But if I let go, I see God using her in people's
lives.

Ellen, mother of Nichole,
who has Down syndrome

My parents went to Sunday worship faithfully, as long as Dad
was able. When he could no longer attend services, the church
family demonstrated Christ's compassion in many ways. Each week,

a different couple visited him during the Sunday school hour. A few faithful men stopped by the house regularly, and later at the nursing home, to keep him company.

But less thoughtful people hurt my parents by twisting God's Word and using it to judge them. The worst offender was a gentleman who told Dad his illness was the consequence of unrepentant sin. Pain and contempt lined Mom's face whenever she mentioned the conversation. "He told your father he wasn't good enough, or God would have cured him."

More than likely you've heard similar remarks from people who have mishandled God's Word. But if no one has accused you, you've probably accused yourself: *I must have done something wrong. God is punishing me. Why can't I make this better?*

Similar thoughts plagued me for months after our son was born. Thanks to a supportive husband and friends who countered lies with truth, the nasty voices gradually faded away. Still, it was years before I recognized both my personal struggle with guilt *and* the judgmental comments of others for what they were—spiritual warfare, the enemy at work.

Truth or Lie

Satan, the enemy of believers, can't take away our salvation. Instead, he tries to weaken our faith and witness by making us feel guilty. Whether the guilt is warranted or not, he uses it to push us into depression, discouragement, and despair. When we succumb to guilt, we fall into sin easily. Even if we don't give in to temptation, our time is spent fighting against it.

The enemy also uses guilt to rob parents of the energy and confidence required for special needs caregiving. If parents falsely believe that they caused their child's condition, they will lack the confidence to discipline wisely. They won't boldly advocate for their child. Nor will they be the example of courageous, joyful faith their children need.

To battle guilt, you first must be able to recognize it. Here are some of its common manifestations:

- *Self-blame:* This is my fault. What did I do wrong?
- *"If only" statements:* If only I'd known more, this wouldn't have happened. If only I'd gotten there faster. If only I'd tried harder.
- *Self-condemning thoughts:* I'm a bad parent. My kids would be better off with someone else.

Once you recognize guilty thoughts, you need to decide whether your sense of guilt is founded in truth or lies. Most likely the latter is true, but sometimes the thoughts contain a kernel of truth. How do you determine which is which?

Start by asking God to reveal the truth to you. Consult His Word. Can you find anything in it to confirm your guilt, or does His truth release you from it? Is your sense of guilt based on disobedience, or is it based on a misconception about Scripture? After consulting God's Word, seek the counsel of someone you trust, perhaps your spouse, a wise family member, or a pastor. Talk about your thoughts, share what Scripture showed you, and ask for advice.

How to Discern between Founded and Unfounded Guilt

1. Ask God to reveal the truth.
2. See what His Word says about the matter.
3. Look for evidence of disobedience.
4. Look for evidence of a misconception.
5. Seek the counsel of someone you trust.

If you both agree your guilt is the result of sin, confess your wrongdoing to God and ask for forgiveness in Christ. Do what is necessary and biblical to change the behavior. Then leave the sin and the guilt behind.

More likely, you will discover the guilty thoughts are unfounded. Expose the lie for the falsehood it is and refuse to believe it. Be prepared for the enemy to attack again, to whisper the same falsehood. When he does, let truth be your weapon. Recite the Scriptures that revealed the lie. Repeat the words of assurance shared by those who gave you counsel. Pray when you sense another attack, and ask others to pray for you, too. And be aware of common misconceptions that make parents of kids with special needs feel guilty.

Guilt and Grief

One common misconception is to confuse grief with guilt. Elizabeth Kubler-Ross defined the five stages of grief in 1969: denial, anger, bargaining, depression, and acceptance. According to Kubler-Ross, guilt is anger turned inward, so it's no surprise that grief is often mislabeled as guilt.

Parents can be ashamed of the grief they feel for their children. They grieve lost dreams, not a lost life. They tell themselves they're being selfish or insensitive to parents of children who died because their children are still alive. They don't recognize that their grief is valid and genuine. When their sadness doesn't go away, they feel increasingly guilty.

Grieving for lost dreams is part of parenting kids with special needs. It is real and valid. When you are sad, don't call your grief guilt and try to bury it. Call it what it is. Expect it, acknowledge it, and allow it.

When your sadness flows from grief rooted in loss, you are in good company. Jesus mourned when Lazarus died, though He knew He would raise him from the dead. He wept when he saw Mary and Martha grieving for their brother. Since Jesus wept, so can you.

Perfection and Imperfection

A second misconception and source of guilt is a false standard of perfection. When a new baby is born with ten fingers, ten toes, and the outward appearance of a typical infant, we say, "She's perfect!" But when a child is born with a special need, we say, "Something's wrong." Immediately, parents wonder if they caused the imperfection. But since when is the form and function of human bodies our standard of perfection?

In Romans, Paul says we've all sinned and come short of the glory of God. He makes it clear that the true standard of perfection is God, not humanity. According to Scripture, even people with ten fingers, ten toes, flawless complexions, full intellectual capacities, and all their innards in the right places are not perfect. Yet we say the baby with all systems go is perfect, but the child born with a cleft palate, developmental delays, or cerebral palsy is not. How cruel we are. And how wrong.

In *Disability and the Church*, Dr. Jeff McNair explains how to avoid a false standard of perfection: "I can choose a standard of perfection that I will succeed at and then use that as my plumb line, or I can use the plumb line that God provides for success and align myself with that. The notion of perfect and imperfect looks quite different when I align myself with God's notion of success or perfect."

Once we make God the true standard of perfection, we see ourselves and others as imperfect. When you see every person on earth as imperfect, you no longer feel guilty about your child's imperfections. They may be different than those of most people. They may be more noticeable or limiting, but your child is no less perfect than anyone else.

Making God the only standard of perfection will help you combat guilt, but it won't end the battle. Whether they were relatively new Christians or mature believers, the parents interviewed for this book said they wage a constant war with guilt. So before moving on to the next chapter, here are a few more weapons for the battle.

Dispelling and Defeating Guilt

Understanding Your Job: One way to dispel guilt is to classify which areas of your child's life are in your care and which are in God's care. Once you know who's in charge of what, you can concentrate on your duties and let God take care of the rest. I learned this lesson during our son's first year of life. For months I battled constant guilt because I couldn't perform two basic mommy tasks: I couldn't protect my baby from the pain of surgery and other invasive medical procedures, and I couldn't hold him close during feedings because his nourishment went through a feeding tube. No wonder I felt inadequate!

Slowly, God taught me two important truths. First, He didn't expect me to do something circumstances wouldn't allow. He expected only what was possible for me to do. Though I couldn't protect Allen from painful medical procedures, I could stay by his side and comfort him afterward. I couldn't nurse Allen, but I could cuddle him after tube feedings.

Second, God expected me to trust Him with what I couldn't control. I had to trust that He would deal with the trauma caused by the frequent pain my baby endured. I had to trust Him to fill any void created when I couldn't cuddle Allen skin to skin. Once I left God's job to Him and concentrated on my job responsibilities, my guilt eased considerably. Yours will too.

Trusting God's Purpose: Believing God has a purpose for you and your child on this special needs journey is another way to combat guilt. In Exodus 4:11, God says, "And who do you think made the human mouth? And who makes some mute, some deaf, some sighted, some blind? Isn't it I, God?"

Here's what Randy Alcorn says about that verse: "Remarkably, God takes full credit for giving these disabilities. God doesn't say the Fall makes people deaf or Satan makes them blind, but that *he* does . . . Right-thinking believers find great comfort in knowing that such life-altering abnormalities don't happen randomly or because of bad luck, but are granted to us with divine purpose. God doesn't helplessly watch us suffer because of bad genes or an accident that Satan or people caused. He offers us help dealing with any disability he's given us."

According to Exodus 4:11, God created your child with a special need. Therefore, He has a reason for it. Maybe He's already revealed what it is. Maybe He's given you only the faintest inkling. Maybe you're still waiting for His purpose to be revealed. But your weapon against guilt isn't how much you understand about God's purpose. Your weapon is a rock hard belief that He has a divine purpose for your child, whether or not you understand what it is.

Praying Scripture: As was mentioned earlier in this chapter, truth is essential in the war against guilt. Therefore, praying Scripture, the source of truth, is the ultimate weapon when guilt attacks.

Where should you start? How should you pray? Many of the psalms were written by people struggling with despair and discouragement, crying out in the midst of disappointment, loss, and uncertainty. Does that sound familiar?

You can turn to the book of Psalms and start with Psalm 1, or you can read until you find a psalm that resonates with your state of mind. An example of how to pray through a psalm is found on the next page. First you'll see the original psalm. Then you'll see how I used it to pray for my son.

Prayer and Reflection

If you want to venture beyond the book of Psalms, consult the prayer guides located in appendix A. Each guide uses passages from the Old and New Testaments. After you pray, spend some time reflecting on what God is saying to you.

Now that you're armed and dangerous—at least in the eyes of our enemy—move on to your next parenting challenge.

Praying through Psalm 139:13–17

Oh yes, you shaped me first inside, then out; you formed me in my mother's womb. I thank you, High God—you're breathtaking! Body and soul, I am marvelously made! I worship in adoration—what a creation! You know me inside and out, you know every bone in my body; You know exactly how I was made, bit by bit, how I was sculpted from nothing into something. Like an open book, you watched me grow from conception to birth; all the stages of my life were spread out before you, The days of my life all prepared before I'd even lived one day. Your thoughts—how rare, how beautiful! God, I'll never comprehend them!

Oh yes, you shaped Allen first inside, then out; you formed him in my womb. I thank you, High God—you're breathtaking! Body and soul, my son is marvelously made! I worship in adoration—what a creation! You know him inside and out, you know every bone in his body; You know exactly how he was made, even his tracheoesophageal fistula, bit by bit, how he was sculpted from nothing into something. Like an open book, you watched him grow from conception to birth; all the stages of his life were spread out before you, The days of his life—all his surgeries and procedures and treatments—all prepared before he'd even lived one day. Your thoughts—how rare, how beautiful! God, I'll never comprehend them! But I will trust them and your purposes for my life and for my son's.

God of truth, I am weary of this constant battle with guilt. Too often the enemy whispers lies to me. Despair and discouragement drain my energy. Show me how to use your Word to combat the enemy so I have energy and confidence to meet the needs of the child you've placed in my care.

What truths of Scripture can help me combat guilt? What misconceptions have created unfounded guilt in my life? What divine purposes do I see God working in my life and my child's? How will I pray Scripture as a weapon against guilt?

Take Time to Reflect

Resources

- Elisabeth Kubler-Ross, *On Death and Dying* (Scribner Classics, 1997).
- Jeff McNair, *The Church and Disability* (CreateSpace, 2010).
- Randy Alcorn, *If God Is Good: Faith in the Midst of Suffering and Evil* (Multnomah, 2009).

Losing a Child

From Loss to Comfort

17

Comfort When Saying Good-bye

"While the child was alive," he said, "I fasted and wept, thinking God might have mercy on me and the child would live. But now that he's dead, why fast? Can I bring him back now? I can go to him, but he can't come to me."

2 Samuel 12:22–23

Our son lived a full life.

Brittany, mother of Michael Anthony, who lived for fifteen days

*K*urt and Joy's fourth living child, Sam, was born on November 18, 2009. His parents had known about his congenital heart condition, hypoplastic left heart syndrome, since mid-August. Sam was delivered at Mayo Clinic, where his older brother Matt receives treatment for his heart condition. Baby Sam fought to live for seventy-two

187

days, and then fell asleep in the arms of his parents. Kurt and Joy say their baby "awoke in the safe embrace of his heavenly Father" on January 29, 2010.

Family members left behind: Kurt, Joy, Parker, Matthew, Emma, and Ben

Military couple Don and Victoria lived in the Middle East during her pregnancy in 2001. When Victoria's pregnancy was at thirty-six weeks, they flew to a hospital in Germany to await their baby's arrival. A stress test revealed complications and doctors performed an emergency cesarean section. When Isaac was born, weighing just three pounds, he was diagnosed with Trisomy 18, a condition caused by a chromosomal abnormality. Don and Victoria spent eleven days loving and caring for their son before they surrendered him to God's hands.

Family members left behind: Don and Victoria

Brian and DeAnn welcomed Andrew, their third child and only son, into the world in 1992. He was a happy and healthy baby until age one, when he was diagnosed with brain cancer. For the next two years, surgery, chemo, and radiation were a regular part of Andrew's life until the cancer went into remission. When the tumor mutated and returned, Brian and DeAnn prayed about what treatment options to pursue. Finally, they decided to let God do what He would. Two months later, God took three-year-old Andrew home.

Family members left behind: Brian, DeAnn, Kerrie, Kristin, and Kacie

Mike and Brittany learned they were expecting in July of 2008. In November, an ultrasound revealed their son's fatal condition. Doctors told them to go home to wait for Brittany to miscarry. But

Brittany didn't miscarry. So they researched the condition and prepared to parent their child for as long as God allowed. Michael was born on March 3, 2009, with an extremely rare genetic condition. His daddy and mommy spent two weeks parenting him in St. Mary's NICU at the Mayo Clinic. Then they made the difficult decision to forego further surgery and sing him home to Jesus. A day later, little Michael passed away. Mike says, "We consider this experience the hardest, but most enriching time of our lives."

Family members left behind: Mike, Brittany, and new baby sister Annabelle

From Hope to Comfort

What is more devastating to parents than the death of a child? However long the parents have known their child—only in utero, for a few short minutes or hours after birth, for weeks or months, for years or decades—their child's death is heartbreaking and feels unnatural. Children should outlive their parents. As the four stories above demonstrate, that doesn't always happen.

If you are reading these chapters, you may have already said good-bye to a child you dearly love. Or maybe you're preparing for that painful reality. Either way, you are walking a difficult and holy path, one I haven't traveled, and my heart aches for you.

In the next four chapters, families who have lost children will share their stories, along with grief and bereavement professionals who will offer their expertise.

This chapter discusses how to care for a terminally ill child and make difficult choices. The next chapter focuses on the tasks, resources, and decisions that arise after the death of a beloved child. Chapter 19 examines the grieving process, and chapter 20 considers voicing doubts and troubling emotions before God.

My prayer is that the witnesses of these families will bring you comfort, hope, and renewed faith. Comfort as you rest in the presence of others who understand your deep pain and loss. Hope in the stories of God using their children and families in unexpected, powerful ways. Renewed faith as the God of all comfort comforts you through the life and death of His Son, Jesus Christ.

With that prayer in mind, we'll review resources that nurture families of children with terminal diagnoses.

Support for Families

Parents need constant, compassionate encouragement after a terminal diagnosis is made. While extended family, friends, and pastors offer support, their lack of experience, along with their own uncertainty and grief, often leaves them unable to meet the needs of immediate family members adequately. In those cases, parents are wise to seek the expertise and compassion offered through pediatric hospice care.

The field of pediatric hospice is continually changing as new medical advances redefine its boundaries. Many children with conditions initially diagnosed as terminal are surviving for years and even decades. In recognition of these changing circumstances, most children's hospitals use the term "palliative care" rather than "children's hospice."

Pain and palliative care teams administer more than end-of-life care. They treat children for pain or other distressing symptoms, and the team can help families track and synthesize a child's care over time, manage emotions, and provide practical tools for everyday life. Stacy Remke, the coordinator for Children's Institute for Pain and Palliative Care at Children's Hospitals and Clinics of Minnesota, says that the focus of palliative care is on comfort and quality of life for children with life-threatening conditions. They also offer end-of-life care for children and families who will soon be separated by death.

Pediatric palliative care services are available to patients at large children's hospitals. For children being treated at smaller medical centers, palliative care professionals may be harder to locate. On the next page are several suggestions about how to find the services you need.

How to Locate Pediatric Pain and Palliative Care Services

- Talk to the hospital chaplain or social worker.
- Call the nearest children's hospital and ask to be transferred to the Palliative Care or Pediatric Hospice Department.
- Go to the website of the children's hospital closest to you and search for these terms: "palliative care," "pediatric hospice," "grief services," "bereavement services."
- Contact one of these national Pediatric Pain and Palliative Care Organizations:
  Children's Hospice and Palliative Care Coalition: http://www.childrenshospice.org/
  National Hospice and Palliative Care Organization: www.nhpco.org/pediatrics
  National Network for Pediatric Palliative Care: http://www.network4pedspallcare.org/
  Perinatal Hospice and Palliative Care: http://perinatalhospice.org

Because many young parents have never experienced the death of a close family member, hospice or palliative care teams walk them through the emotions they will experience, provide needed care, give information about planning a funeral, and advise them about state rules and regulations.

Most importantly, they help parents prepare their children for death by encouraging families to live each day fully and create lasting memories. On the next page several parents describe how they made memories in their children's final days.

Support through Memories

In interview after interview, parents mentioned the importance of creating both mementos and memories with their children.

During Michael's fifteen days of life, his dad snapped over eight hundred photos. Michael's mother, Brittany, admits it wasn't easy to take pictures. She advises parents, "Force yourselves to do it. If you don't, you'll wish you had."

Their hospital offered other memory-making opportunities. They were given boxes for locks of Michael's hair. Someone made plaster casts of their son's tiny hands and feet. A professional photographer took pictures. Scrapbook supplies were available for parents who wanted to make memory books. "I encourage parents to take advantage of these things," Brittany says.

Sheila Frascht, coordinator of grief services at the University of Iowa Children's Hospital, explains the importance of such mementos: "They are a layer of support that helps parents gain control and make the experience meaningful. Handprints, footprints, and photographs give parents a tangible bond with their child." More information about documenting memories can be found in the resource section at the end of this chapter.

Other memory-making opportunities exist for older children. The Make-a-Wish Foundation arranges once-in-a-lifetime experiences for children with serious or terminal illnesses. Kids and their families visit places like Disney World or Space Camp, meet celebrities, attend sports events, and more. Go to www.wish.org to find the chapter nearest you.

The best memories aren't necessarily the spectacular ones. DeAnn remembers one of Andrew's birthday parties as a happy time. Mike and Brittany find comfort when they think about how they read the book of John aloud to Michael in the NICU. "It was part of our parenting. It was something we could do."

What comfort these simple memories will provide for years to come. What grace for dads and moms to know they gave their child a full life. What joy to recall the comfort and security their presence brought to their child.

Support for Dying Children

Creating memories while a child is alive brings great comfort to the family members left behind. But sometimes, onlookers misinterpret the family's acceptance and preparation for death as a lack of faith in God's ability to heal miraculously. They pressure parents to pray for healing instead. Nancy, who lost two children, Hope and Gabriel, believes parents should be released from such expectations. She says, "Sometimes people become aggressive, urging families to pray for healing miracles. If the parents talk about death, they're accused of doubting God. But if the reality of death is ignored, the family is robbed of the chance for memorable, meaningful conversation with the dying person."

Nancy suggests parents look for opportunities to talk with their children about what's happening. "If a child faces death, what a gift it is to have a conversation. Not about 'you're dying,' but 'you're in God's hands.'" She recommends comforting and preparing a child by talking about these known truths:

- God can be trusted.
- God will do what is right for you.
- We will miss you.
- The time we'll be apart is a tiny blip in eternity.
- We look forward to spending eternity with you illness-free.

How to communicate those truths and in how much depth depends on the age and maturity level of your child.

If you are unsure about how to talk to your child about death, ask pain and palliative care team members or hospice workers for guidance. They have training and experience that helps them broach the subject with children of all ages. Stacy Remke says, "We see patterns and themes emerge that can comfort families and children. Even young children give clues that they know what's going on. We try to bring that out by asking, 'What are you feeling?' or 'What are you thinking about?'"

Parents can also use age-appropriate books to prepare a terminally ill child for what lies ahead. Through fictional characters, children can process death from a comfortable distance, and then apply and internalize what they've learned to their own lives.

Book recommendations for kids of different ages can be found in the resource section at the end of this chapter. Your pain and palliative care team may have more suggestions. They may even have a lending library. To help you select appropriate books, the sidebar describes features of books geared to different ages.

Many beloved children's classics can prompt meaningful discussions about loss and death. By reading them together, not only will you create a lasting, meaningful memory, but also a safe haven where your child can ask questions and voice concerns.

Talking about eternity can be a great comfort to children who are dying. Randy Alcorn's book *Heaven* is a comprehensive look at what the Bible says about the afterlife. Alcorn answers the questions we often hesitate to ask. In *Heaven for Kids*, Alcorn uses selected content from *Heaven* to answer questions of interest to kids. He begins with "Why should we look forward to heaven?" Then the discussion moves on to what elementary-aged kids are curious about, including "Will we sleep?" "Might some animals talk?" and "Will there be sports?" A picture book version, *Tell Me about Heaven*, is appropriate for younger children.

The resources and organizations mentioned in this chapter can help siblings of a dying child, too. By reading them fiction books that touch on death, you give siblings permission to talk about the subject. Pain and palliative care team members are trained to work with siblings, so take advantage of their expertise and recommendations.

The bookstore at SibShops (http://astore.amazon.com/thesibsup pro-20) has many resources geared to siblings.

Characteristics of Age-Appropriate Fiction Books

Ages 2–4
Short picture books

Death issues are faced and discussed by animals.

Ages 5–8
Longer picture books

Main characters are children dealing with the death of a pet, grandparent, or elderly friend.

Ages 9–12
Chapter books

Main characters are children dealing with the death of a close family member or friend.

Ages 13+
Young adult fiction or adult fiction

Main characters are teens or adults dealing with the death of a loved one or facing their own death.

Support for Where You Are

During this difficult time, take advantage of the resources designed to support families experiencing great loss. Lean on the professionals trained to help you. Parent without regrets. Make memories. Take pictures. Read to your children. Answer questions. Speak truth. Do what you *can* do, so when your child leaves your care, you will echo Brittany's words: "My child lived a full life."

Dear God of life and bearer of our sadness, our family is living in a place we do not want to be. We are heartbroken, wishing we could wake up and discover our situation is a bad dream. But it isn't a dream. This is real. Give us strength and wisdom to parent our child to the end of a full and victorious life.

Which family members and friends will support the way we parent our dying child? What role do we want the pain and palliative care team to play? What clues show that our child wants to discuss death? How can we prepare for the discussion?

Take Time to Reflect

Resources

Hospice and Palliative Care Organizations

- Children's Hospice and Palliative Care Coalition: www.childrenshospice.org
- Children's Hospice International: www.chionline.org
- National Hospice and Palliative Care Organization: www.nhpco.org/pediatrics
- National Network for Pediatric Palliative Care: www.network 4pedspallcare.org

- Perinatal Hospice and Palliative Care: www.perinatalhospice .org

Memory-Making Resources

- Now I Lay Me Down to Sleep: www.nowilaymedowntosleep .org/home
- American Child Photographers Charity Guild: www.acpcg .org
- Memorial Jewelry: www.funeral-urn.com/thumbies-memorial -jewelry.aspx
- Make-a-Wish Foundation: www.wish.org

Books for Parents

- Randy Alcorn, *Heaven* (Tyndale, 2004).
- Nancy Guthrie, *Holding onto Hope: A Pathway through Suffering to the Heart of God* (Tyndale, 2006).

Books for Siblings

- SibShops bookstore: http://astore.amazon.com/thesibsuppro-20

Books for Young Children

- Randy Alcorn, *Tell Me About Heaven* (Crossway, 2007).
- Laurie Brown and Mike Brown, *When Dinosaurs Die: A Guide to Understanding Death* (Little, Brown Books for Young Readers, 1998).
- Leo Buscaglia, *The Fall of Freddie the Leaf* (Slack Incorporated, 1982).
- Carolyn Nystrom, *What Happens When We Die?* (Children's Bible Basics, 2003).
- Beverly Lewis, *What Is Heaven Like?* (Bethany House, 2006).

Books for Tweens and Teens

- Randy Alcorn, *Heaven for Kids* (Tyndale Kids, 2006).
- C. S. Lewis, *The Last Battle* (HarperCollins, 2000)
- Barbara Parks, *Mick Hart Was Here* (Yearling, 1996).
- Marjorie Rawlings, *The Yearling* (Aladdin Classics, 2001).
- Wilson Rawls, *Where the Red Fern Grows* (Perfection Learning, 1997).
- Gary Schmidt, *Lizzie Bright and the Buckminster Boy* (Laurel Leaf, 2008).
- Gary Schmidt, *Trouble* (Graphia, 2010).
- E. B. White, *Charlotte's Web* (HarperCollins, 2001).
- Laura Ingalls Wilder, *By the Shores of Silver Lake* (Harper Collins, 2004).

18

Comfort in the Details

The king was stunned. Heartbroken, he went up to
the room over the gate and wept. As he wept he
cried out, "O my son Absalom, my dear, dear son
Absalom! Why not me rather than you, my death
and not yours, O Absalom, my dear, dear son!"

2 Samuel 18:33

Planning a funeral is nothing a parent should ever
have to do for a child. It's beyond heartbreaking.

Joy, mother of Sam,
who lived seventy-two days

A few days before our fifteen-year-old son was scheduled for major
surgery in December of 1997, a thought came to mind during my
morning devotions.

You need to let Allen plan his funeral.

I squelched the idea, chalking it up to my overly dramatic nature,
and went on with my day. But that night while drifting off to sleep,
the thought returned.

Let Allen plan his funeral.

This time, I raised a few objections. *And how am I supposed to do that, God? Go up to my son and say, "Hey, buddy, since your major surgery is just around the corner, how about you leave funeral instructions in case the surgeon's knife slips?"*

God didn't answer immediately, and I finally fell asleep. The next morning, I mentioned the idea to my husband. He nodded. "We should talk to him tonight."

In the evening, Hiram and I waited in the living room. I mentally rehearsed several conversation openers, but none of them grabbed me. *I sure hope Hiram has something up his sleeve.*

Allen entered the room and sat down, his face serious. "Dad. Mom." He looked at us in turn. "I want to plan my funeral. In case I don't make it through the surgery. Will you help?" We nodded. Grateful for God's grace in having Allen initiate the conversation, I tried to listen to our son's words. However, two reoccurring thoughts kept me from concentrating: *This conversation shouldn't be happening. My son shouldn't be planning his own funeral.*

But it was happening. Our son, a freshman in high school, was telling us who he wanted to conduct his funeral service, what music should be played, and what clothes he wanted to be buried in. Tears still come to my eyes when I picture our son earnestly confronting his own mortality. Though Allen lived, the wrongness of the topic of conversation and the rightness of having the conversation are truths that live inside me.

For parents reading this chapter, similar discussions will become part of who you are. Your child is dying or has died. A funeral must be planned. A precious life is to be honored. And you, like many other parents in your situation, do not know where to begin. This chapter is your starting point.

How to Begin

Many people dedicate their lives to assisting families in your situation. Depending on your circumstances, your first contact could be a hospital chaplain, the hospital palliative care team or hospice worker, a bereavement counselor, or a church pastor.

If the situation allows, some parents make plans while their child is still living. The last three weeks of Andrew's life gave his parents, Brian and DeAnn, that opportunity. "He had one good week, then a week when he was uncomfortable, and then a week in a coma," DeAnn remembers. "The last week gave us time to plan." When Andrew died, his parents were relieved knowing details were handled.

"Other families want to wait until the last minute," says Stacy Remke, a coordinator for Children's Institute for Pain and Palliative Care at Children's Hospitals and Clinics of Minnesota. End-of-life care providers let parents know that resources are available, provide general guidance, and wait until families are ready for more specific planning.

When you're ready to plan, ask for help. If someone already gave you information but you're fuzzy about the details or can't remember where the paperwork is, ask again. No one will mind. They know the stress you are under. They want to support you.

Brian Brooks, the head chaplain at the Children's Hospitals and Clinics of Minnesota, often assists parents with tasks. "We chaplains make the initial call to the funeral home once the family has chosen a location. The family has to make the arrangements, but we can help them prepare the service."

If your child isn't hospitalized or receiving support from a palliative care team, your church pastor or the funeral home personnel can assist you. Even if your child wasn't in a hospital, contact the chaplain at the nearest hospital or children's hospital. They can tell you where to begin, and they can connect you to people and resources you need.

How to Prepare for a Funeral

Joy's words about baby Sam earlier in this chapter are true. The loss of a child is beyond heartbreaking. Planning a child's funeral is something a parent should never have to do. If it is your reality, rest assured that God can use the service to honor your precious child and begin healing your broken heart.

Your pastor or the funeral directors will walk you through the basic components of a funeral service. Rather than discuss them here, we'll move on to questions specific to parents and families.

Should the Child Be Involved in Planning? If your child is old enough to understand she's dying, she may want—or even need—to participate in planning the funeral. But how do you bring up the subject to learn her wishes?

Once again, remember that you are the expert on your child. If you think your child understands what is happening, she probably does. If your child has definite opinions and likes to voice them in family discussions, then she probably wants to be heard in this discussion, too.

Chaplain Brooks says some elementary-aged kids will initiate the conversation by asking parents what will happen at their funeral. He suggests answering creatively. Use art, books, or music to continue the discussion without overwhelming a child. Give a small piece of information about funerals, and then let them steer the conversation.

When talking to preteens and teenagers, treat them as adults. Listening to your child's last wishes may not be easy, but it is essential. If they have preferences, honor them as you would those of a dying adult. By respecting their decisions, you are giving your child the gifts of adulthood and closure. Honoring their wishes is essential for your mental health, too. It allows you to live without regrets or doubts. You won't wonder if things should have been done differently because you followed your child's requests.

What Will Siblings Do? Brothers and sisters old enough to understand what's happening may want to help plan and participate in the service. Chaplain Brooks says, "It's important to give siblings a sense of control. Let them make decisions and choose their level of involve-

Ways to Involve Siblings

Younger Siblings

Pick out songs or sing

Select pictures for a memory board or slide show

Hand out order of service and obituary

Write and/or read a poem

Older Siblings

Play an instrument

Make a memory board or slide show

Serve as a pallbearer

Speak at the service

Adapted from *How to Plan a Funeral* by Liz Cowen Furman

ment. Give them choices. Would they like to visit the dying child in the hospital or write letters instead?"

After their brother or sister dies, give the siblings choices about their participation in the service. Don't overwhelm them—offer a few suggestions and allow them time to think them over or come up with something else. "Ways to Involve Siblings" has ideas your kids can consider and adapt.

Funeral or Celebration? Another consideration is deciding what to call the service. The name you choose is meaningful. Mike and Brittany chose to call Michael's service "a celebration service" because it reflected their hope. Brittany says, "We had a celebration service for

Michael at the church. We didn't have a viewing, because our son was gone. As soon as Michael passed away, I didn't cling to him. I differentiated between our son and his body."

Mike and Brittany chose a significant verse from Job 1:21 for the celebration: "Naked I came from my mother's womb, And naked I shall return there. The Lord gave and the Lord has taken away. Blessed be the name of the Lord" (NASB).

"We highlighted the 'blessed be the name of the Lord' part of the verse," Brittany says. They deliberately emphasized their belief in life beyond death, a life in the presence of the Lord who gave them Michael and gently, compassionately took him away.

The songs they chose reflected their hope: "It Is Well with My Soul," "Great Is Thy Faithfulness," "Softly and Tenderly," and "I Surrender All." They also chose "Jesus Loves Me," a song they sang over and over to Michael during his life, as a way to celebrate the memory of parenting him.

Sherry and Kevin said good-bye to their seven-month-old daughter, Audrey Grace, when Trisomy 18 complications ended her life. Sherry describes how they planned the service: "I didn't plan it until we lost her. I just couldn't. After she left us for heaven, I picked aunts and uncles to read poems, and I put together a slide show to the Steven Curtis Chapman song 'With Hope.' The lyrics are so powerful for a parent who has lost a child."

Audrey Grace's parents called their daughter's service a Celebration of Life. Sherry's hope-filled perspective came from knowing Audrey Grace is whole and happy, free from pain, fully restored, and safe under the watchful eye of the Creator. She says, "Audrey is being healed of having a caterpillar body here on earth and is getting to be a heavenly butterfly with a body unencumbered by defects."

Sherry used the service to preserve and share her daughter's life history with others, a history grounded in the hope of eternal life.

How to Find Hope

The death of a child is devastating. Planning a child's funeral is heartbreaking. But your child's life was a precious gift, worthy of celebration. I pray your child's service will be a hope and comfort to all who loved your child. I pray the memories you create while honoring your child's life may sustain you in your grief.

Dear Jesus, planning a funeral is so hard. We are bereft and broken. We are grieving. Our child's life was precious, worthy, valuable. Give us strength to plan a service that acknowledges our grief, rejoices in the days we shared together, and looks ahead to the hope of eternal life in you.

Can we help our child prepare for death through planning the funeral? Who can show us what to do? How do our living children want to participate? How can the service bring hope to our family and others attending?

Take Time to Reflect

Resources

Books

- Liz Cowen Furman, *How to Plan a Funeral: And Other Things You Need to Know When a Loved One Dies* (Beacon Hill, 2008).

- *What about the Kids? Understanding Their Needs in Funeral Planning and Services* (The Dougy Center). To order, go to www.dougy .org and pull down the "Books and DVDs" tab.

General Resources

- Lyrics to "With Hope" by Steven Curtis Chapman: http:// www.christianlyricsonline.com/artists/steven-curtis-chapman /with-hope.html
- Memorial cards: www.babydekar.com/memorial-cardsbirth -announcements
- Guidelines for planning a child's funeral: www.americanhospice .org/articles-mainmenu-8/grieving-children-mainmenu-12/63 -guidelines-for-planning-a-childrens-funeral
- Pregnancy and infant loss memorial planning: www.national share.org/memorial-planning.html

19

Comfort in Grief

> For my dear broken people, I'm heartbroken. I
> weep, seized by grief.
>
> Jeremiah 8:21
>
> If parents can accept the love and support others
> offer, it will help on their grief journey. It's hard to
> do when you're hurting, but it helps.
>
> Brian Brooks, head chaplain,
> Children's Hospitals and Clinics of Minnesota

Our family was prepared for Dad's death in 1997. He'd been ill with multiple sclerosis (MS) for almost four decades and in a nursing home for fourteen years. His declining health and long suffering were an inexorable grief to my siblings and my mom. Year after year, we mourned while MS slowly ravaged his body and mind.

We were more than prepared for Dad's death. We were relieved by it. Finally, Dad's suffering was over. He was in heaven, whole again, himself again, no doubt talking a mile a minute after a long spell of silence, when he could whisper no more than a word to visitors.

I had mourned often during Dad's later years, each time he didn't know my name or recognize his grandchildren. So I didn't expect the onslaught of emotion after his death. It hit whenever my kids and I did things my father's illness didn't allow him to do with me. Tears flowed during my morning walks, and I thought of how many years Dad sat in a wheelchair. Even today, I keep a box of tissues nearby when writing about my sweet, sad memories of Dad.

Elisabeth Kubler-Ross and David Kessler's words in *On Grief and Grieving* ring true with my experience: "The reality is that you will grieve forever. You will not 'get over' the loss of a loved one; you will learn to live with it. You will heal, and you will rebuild yourself around the loss you have suffered. You will be whole again, but you will never be the same."

I am not the person I was before the loss of my father, just as you are not the person you were before you lost your child. You will never be that person again. If your loss is recent and your heart is still an open wound, you may be skeptical about promises of healing and wholeness someday. But God will keep His promises as you embrace your grief. You will begin to heal.

The grief journey will be uniquely yours, but it will share some similarities with the journeys of others. You will cycle through the five stages of grief defined by Elisabeth Kubler-Ross. In this chapter we'll look at those stages, along with concerns common to grieving parents and siblings. Once again, parents and professionals will walk beside you, sharing their experiences and advice along the way.

Stages of Grief

Kubler-Ross first identified the five stages of grief in her 1969 book, *On Death and Dying*, explaining their manifestation in terminally ill people. She wrote extensively on the subjects of death and grief for three decades. In her last book, *On Grief and Grieving*, she once again examined the five stages of grief, this time in relation to the people left behind. Her observations are summarized below.

Denial: When people learn they are dying, they deny the truth by saying, "Maybe the tests were wrong," or "This can't be happening." For those grieving the loss of a loved one, the manifestation of denial is slightly different. Grieving people don't deny a loved one's death. Instead, they find it hard to believe the loved one is no longer a part of their routine. A mother can't believe she won't clean her son's trach tube any more. A dad waits for the bus to drop off his daughter after school, unable to believe he doesn't need to push her wheelchair up the driveway.

Denial prevents the implications of a death from becoming too overwhelming. Through denial, a person can deal with the loss in manageable, though painful, bits. Numbness and shock accompany this stage. People often repeat the story of their loss, which gradually makes it become real.

Anger: When mourners feel angry, it is a sign that they feel safe enough to survive what comes next. Their anger about the loss may be aimed at medical professionals, the dead person who didn't obey safety instructions, whoever caused the accident, or God for allowing it to happen. Anger is an emotion that hides other feelings beneath it, most often pain. By allowing and expressing anger instead of burying it, the underlying emotions can also be released and healing can continue.

Bargaining: A dying person bargains with God, promising to change in exchange for healing. For those grieving a loss, bargaining takes the form of "if onlys" and "what ifs." Some people return to the past and imagine a different outcome, thus finding a temporary reprieve from pain. The reprieve allows them to suffer at a distance or establishes a temporary sense of control. Over time, the bargaining changes until the mind is finally able to handle the difficult truth: a beloved person is gone.

Depression: Our society perceives depression as an illness in need of treatment. While depression sometimes requires treatment, it is also a natural part of the sadness that accompanies loss. During the depression, life may seem pointless. The grieving person feels lethargic. This stage slows a person down enough to examine the loss. This deep look into the soul is necessary for healing because it prepares the mourner for rebuilding and growth.

Acceptance: In this stage, grieving parents do not "get over" the loss of a child. Instead, they accept that the child is physically gone and learn to live with this new reality. They begin to put life back together, giving themselves new roles and drawing closer to the loved one who died in the process.

Five Stages of Grief

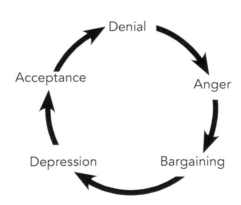

Kubler-Ross says the progression of the five stages has been misrepresented as being linear. In reality, the progression is cyclical. A person doesn't march through the five stages, one right after another, and then complete the grieving process. Instead, people cycle through them, in no particular order, throughout life. Reentry into one of the stages can be triggered by anniversaries, events, and further losses. This is why parents who have lost children never "get over" it. Rather, by recognizing, allowing, and welcoming grief when it returns, healing and rebuilding progresses. Wholeness comes, but the parent is not the same as before the loss occurred.

Parents and Grief

The five stages of grief are universal, but loss impacts people in different ways. Let's take a look at how it can affect parents and siblings.

Role and Routine: For parents of kids with special needs, life revolves around caregiving. When death comes, the absence of the child eliminates the need for established caregiving roles and routines. Parents often feel lost and purposeless. Redefining the self, finding new roles, and creating new routines are major parts of the grieving process.

The only people who truly understand the devastating effect of lost roles and routines are parents who have also lost children. For that reason, a bereavement support group may be of great value to you. Often hospice workers or the pain and palliative care department at children's hospitals sponsor bereavement workshops or support groups. So do online groups specific to certain medical conditions. Compassionate Friends (www.compassionatefriends.org /home) is an international organization with parent support groups in every state and several foreign countries.

Married couples or families may want to consider a retreat. David and Nancy Guthrie conduct Respite (www.nancyguthrie.com /retreats), a retreat for parents who have lost children. Faith's Lodge (www.faithslodge.org), located in northwestern Wisconsin, provides "a place where parents and families facing the serious illness or loss of a child can go to reflect on the past, renew strength for the present, and build hope for the future." They offer professionally led discussion groups, therapeutic arts and crafts, and north woods adventures at no cost to parents and families. Faith's Lodge requires a referral from the hospital healthcare team, faith community, a mental health practitioner, or an approved support organization.

Sex: The loss of a child can build a wall between spouses. Grief makes it hard to communicate true desires. Often, one person's expressed desire for sex is actually a desire for tenderness and closeness.

One mother said she and her husband had sex the evening after their young child died. "It was such a relief after weeks of tension," she explains. Other couples feel guilty for even contemplating the aliveness of lovemaking. Intimacy can be a way to share loss and find comfort, so be sensitive to one another. Talk about how you feel. Avoid judging or condemning your spouse's desire. If the issue can't be resolved, talk to a counselor, before loss of intimacy becomes a casualty to grief.

Special Occasions: Anniversaries, birthdays, holidays, and family traditions can be more than a family can bear after the loss of a child. But ignoring or suppressing the specialness of certain times of the year isn't the answer either. Instead, a way must be forged through the events, one that allows grief but not immobilizing pain.

A friend of mine lost a child in a car accident shortly after Christmas several years ago. The next November, we were chatting in the grocery store and I asked about her holiday plans. "We're going to my sister's in Phoenix," she said. "We want to be with family at Christmas. We're not ready to spend it in our own home without our daughter. Not yet."

They grieved for their daughter that first Christmas, but in a place and a way they and their living children could handle. You too may need distance from special dates or family traditions until you have healed.

Possessions: Deciding what to do with your child's possessions can be heart-wrenching. Sorting through possessions doesn't need to be done immediately, but don't put it off for too long either. For the sake of your living children, never turn the deceased child's room into a shrine. Instead, honor any last wishes your child gave and distribute items according to his directives. Then choose some items for yourself and your spouse, as precious, tangible companions for your grief journey, and allow your living children to select keepsakes. Finally, decide what to do with any remaining items. Consider donating them to charity or passing them on to families that will make good use of them.

Tiffany found a way to handle her grief and pain without creating a shrine for her son. Ethan died of a rare blood disorder a week after his birth. Tiffany keeps some of his clothes in a box because she can't bear to part with the outfits. "I miss what won't be," she says. "Sometimes I open the box of clothes to smell him. It's very hard to be without him, but if I immerse myself in his things, I don't miss him as much."

Guilt: Brian Brooks, a chaplain at Children's Hospitals and Clinics of Minnesota, says guilt is commonly voiced by parents who lose children: "They feel as though they have failed, as though they didn't fulfill a basic parental role. One of the roles of a parent is to fix things, so when they can't fix their child's illness, they think, 'What good am I?' Because mothers are usually the primary caregiver, women may more acutely feel they've failed in their basic role in life."

Parents Feel Guilt Because . . .

- they think they shouldn't be angry.
- they think they failed to strike a bargain with God.
- they're alive and their child isn't.
- they think the death was their fault.

Guilt surfaces during the grieving process in many ways. Some manifestations of guilt are listed in the sidebar. Do any of them sound familiar? During interviews, many parents of kids with special needs said they battled guilt, whether their child lived or died. They talk more about those struggles in chapter 16.

Siblings and Grief

While dealing with their own grief, parents must also help their living children grieve for their sibling. Kubler-Ross says, "Children do not have the resources or experiences to integrate loss into their world. In their minds they often fill in gaps with thoughts like 'It must somehow be my fault.' Unfortunately, the person who should be shepherding them through their grief is the surviving parent, who is often too lost in his or her own grief."

How do you shepherd a child through grief when you are grieving too? Kubler-Ross gives three suggestions:

- Have a series of discussions with your child, not just one. This allows you to clear up misconceptions that may develop as the child tries to fill in the gaps of understanding.
- Inform children ahead of time that they will experience mixed emotions.
- Model grief for children. Tell stories about the child who has died. Use his or her name. Laugh and cry in front of your child. Tell them this is what grief looks like.

Sharing memories with your children is a step toward becoming whole again. DeAnn's son Andrew died when their two older daughters were nine and six. Their third daughter was born after her brother died. DeAnn says, "We talked about Andrew when the girls were younger. We still do. Andrew is part of our family." Your child is and always will be part of your family. Talking about the child you lost is part of living with the loss instead of getting over it.

After the death of her children, Hope and Gabriel, Nancy says she faced a difficult decision: "Would my primary energy go to my dead children or my living child?" Deep in her own grief, she thought, "What if I lose my living child to distance caused by my grief?" Once she chose to focus on the living, she began to pour her energies into loving her son Matt in ways that were meaningful to him.

Parents should look into programs available to grieving siblings. Many children's hospitals hold bereavement workshops. SibShop offers bereavement resources and support groups for siblings, as does

How to Help Siblings Grieve

Do   Allow siblings to be bad and scream sometimes.

Allow siblings to share feelings (even negative ones) about their deceased sibling.

Pay attention to living children.

Talk about the lost sibling as a member of the family.

Don't Pressure siblings to be perfect.

Idealize the deceased child.

Focus completely on your own grief.

Act as if the child never lived or is no longer part of the family.

the Dougy Foundation. If you think your child needs professional counseling, your church pastor, the nearest children's hospital, or your local hospital can recommend practitioners. Pick up the phone and call someone if you need to. In doing so, you'll teach your children another important grief lesson—it's okay to ask for help.

Your Path of Grief

You have experienced a tremendous loss. You must walk this long path of loss, grief, and healing at your own pace. Don't be surprised when you get mad at God. Just make a list of questions for Him. As you'll learn in chapter 20, He's big enough to handle your questions, outlast your anger, and bear your pain. He's big enough to make you whole again.

Dear God, I miss my child so much. Why did you take away what was dearest to me? How will I bear this grief? How can I be the parent my other children need? God, help me. I'm drowning.

How can I talk to other family members about my grief? Who can help us through this? What do my other children need?

Take Time to Reflect

Resources

Books

- Dave Branon, *Beyond the Valley* (Discovery House Publishers, 2010).
- Elisabeth Kubler-Ross and David Kessler, *On Grief and Grieving* (Scribner, 2007).
- David Guthrie and Nancy Guthrie, *When Your Family's Lost a Loved One: Finding Hope Together* (Tyndale, 2008).
- Harold Smith, *Decembered Grief* (Beacon Hill Press, 1999).
- Luke Veldt, *Written in Tears: A Grieving Father's Journey Through Psalm 103* (Discovery House Publishers, 2010).

Online Resources

- Compassionate Friends: www.compassionatefriends.org/home
- David and Nancy Guthrie's Respite Retreat: www.nancy guthrie.com/retreats
- Faith's Lodge: www.faithslodge.org
- The Center for Loss: www.centerforloss.com
- The Dougy Center: www.dougy.org

216

- M.I.S.S. Foundation: www.missfoundation.org/index.html
- National Child Traumatic Stress Network (NCTSN): http://www.nctsn.org/. At the top of the page, pull down the "Trauma Types" menu and click on "Traumatic Grief" to locate the section on sibling death.

20

Comfort in Christ

We don't have a priest who is out of touch with our
reality. He's been through weakness and testing,
experienced it all—all but the sin. So let's walk right
up to him and get what he is so ready to give. Take
the mercy, accept the help.

Hebrews 4:15–16

My advice to parents of a dying child? Cry out to
God.

Brittany, mother of Michael,
who lived fifteen days

The day our young adult son refused to touch me, I was nearly undone by grief. Allen was immature, confused, and struggling with an undiagnosed mental illness. Ignorant of the true cause of his behavior, my heart broke when he refused to hug me and said good-bye with a sad nod instead. I sobbed uncontrollably afterward.

219

As I cried, slowly and unexpectedly a picture of Christ, arms nailed to the cross, filled my inward vision. Then a second picture joined the first: God the Father, His face grief-stricken as He gazed at His Son, His arms hanging at His side. A verse came to mind: "For since He Himself was tempted in that which He has suffered, He is able to come to the aid of those who are tempted" (Hebrews 2:18 NASB).

A whisper stirred my heart. *God knows. The Father knows how it feels to be separated from His Son. And His Son experienced the pain of rejection by the children He loved and came to save. My God knows.*

For years I had marveled at Christ's willing sacrifice on the cross for believers' salvation. But that dark day, I marveled for another reason. Christ suffered pain and sorrow on the cross so I could know that He and the Father understood grief, too.

For a moment, I could barely breathe.

My healing began with that realization. God, the powerful and sovereign Lord, shared my grief and my son's pain. He would help me survive this heartache. I took a deep breath and chose to move on with life, despite the absence of my son from everyday family life.

Please understand, I'm not equating my grief over Allen's rejection with your grief over your child's death. Instead, I am equating your grief with the Father's grief over the death of His Son, with whom He had dwelt in perfect communion since before time began.

God knows your grief. He is waiting for you to cry out to Him, to share your sorrow and pain. Just as He had a great, saving purpose for the loss of His Son, He has a purpose for your loss, too. He will reveal it to you as you walk the path of grief and healing together.

One way He walks with you is through the experiences of other grieving parents who found God faithful throughout their suffering. In this chapter, we'll examine parents in the Bible who lost children and hear from modern-day parents who continue to see God reveal His grand purposes for their children's short lives.

Parents in the Midst of Grief

You don't have to read far in the Old Testament to find parents who lost children. Four chapters into the first book of the Bible, Adam and Eve's oldest son, Cain, murdered Abel, his younger brother. The book of Job tells of a godly man's loss of seven sons and three daughters to a natural disaster. The two books of Samuel tell how David lost three sons. In the Gospels, four different authors recount how God the Father sent His own Son to earth, knowing His life would end on a cross.

The thoughts and emotions of these biblical parents can bring surprising comfort to modern mourners. Many in our contemporary culture insist on maintaining a "stiff upper lip." They erroneously believe Christians must "rejoice always." In contrast, ancient believers exhibited profound and debilitating grief.

Adam and Eve: The Bible doesn't record Adam and Eve's response to their double loss. After Cain killed Abel, God condemned the murderer to a lifetime of wandering. Only one further tidbit about Adam and Eve's story is divulged at the end of Genesis 4: "Adam slept with his wife again. She had a son whom she named Seth. She said, "God has given me another child in place of Abel whom Cain killed" (Genesis 4:25–26). Not much information, but enough to welcome Eve into the company of mothers who have lost children, into the company of parents who carry the memory of their loss as long as they live. Enough to ease your guilt about not being able to fill the empty spot created by the loss of your precious child.

Job: Contrast Adam and Eve's silence about their loss to Job's reaction in Job 1. His reaction is anything but quiet.

> Job got to his feet, ripped his robe, shaved his head, then fell to the ground and worshiped: "Naked I came from my mother's womb, naked I'll return to the womb of the earth. God gives, God takes. God's name be ever

blessed." Not once through all this did Job sin; not once did he blame God. (Job 1:20–22)

Maybe Job didn't blame God, but he sure questioned Him. In the next forty-one chapters, he asks God why, he mourns, and he listens to the advice and chastisement of his friends. Through it all, God doesn't scold Job for asking questions. Instead He commends Job for expressing his emotions honestly while admonishing Eliphaz and his two cohorts: "You haven't been honest either with me or about me—not the way my friend Job has" (Job 42:7).

God acknowledges, even welcomes, Job's expressions of anger, frustration, loss, and despair. God allows Job to ask questions, remaining silent until Job has nothing more to say. But there's one thing God doesn't do. He doesn't answer Job. He never tells him why his children died. Instead God reveals His nature to Job through a series of startling questions, beginning with "Where were you when I created the earth?" (Job 38:4) and ending three chapters later with "Or can you pull in the sea beast, Leviathan, with a fly rod and stuff him in your creel? Can you lasso him with a rope, or snag him with an anchor?" (Job 41:1–2). Job humbly acknowledges God's glory and power: "I'm convinced: You can do anything and everything. Nothing and no one can upset your plans" (Job 42:2).

God never tells Job why he and his children had to suffer. But Job chooses to trust God, believing He is who He says He is—the God who created the earth, the God who can pull sea creatures from the water, the God who gave Job his children as a gift, and the God who took them home.

Since God didn't scold Job for asking hard questions, surely He won't scold you either. Since He welcomed Job's outpouring of honest emotions, surely He will welcome yours, too. But since He chose to reveal His glory to Job instead of explaining why his children died, your most pressing questions may also remain unanswered while your understanding of who God is increases. So ask your questions and express your emotions. Expect God to reveal himself to you on this journey of grief, whether or not He chooses to tell you why He allowed your child to die.

David: The greatest king of Israel, called a man after God's own heart, lost three children. He grieved bitterly after the death of his infant son. Years later, two of David's adult sons, Amnon and Absalom, quarreled. By the end of the fight, Amnon was dead, killed by Absalom. Later, Absalom died in battle after trying to usurp his father's throne. Though Absalom's crimes were numerous, David's grief for his rebel child nearly incapacitated him.

David's grief for his infant son, born into less than perfect circumstances, is raw and desperate. The child was conceived during the king's illicit love affair with Bathsheba. To cover his sin, David sent Bathsheba's husband, Uriah, to the front lines of battle where he was killed. David then married Bathsheba and their son was born. When confronted with his sin, David confessed it to God, repented, and received forgiveness. Soon after David and Bathsheba's newborn baby became deathly ill, and David cried out to God:

> David prayed desperately to God for the little boy. He fasted, wouldn't go out, and slept on the floor. The elders in his family came in and tried to get him off the floor, but he wouldn't budge. Nor could they get him to eat anything. (2 Samuel 12:16–17)

As long as his son was alive, David did everything he could to save him. David was so distraught that his servants feared what he would do when he learned of his son's death. Here is David's surprising response:

> David got up from the floor, washed his face and combed his hair, put on a fresh change of clothes, then went into the sanctuary and worshiped. Then he came home and

asked for something to eat. They set it before him and he ate. (2 Samuel 12:20)

When his servants asked him to explain his reaction, he said,

While the child was alive, . . . I fasted and wept, thinking God might have mercy on me and the child would live. But now that he's dead, why fast? Can I bring him back now? I can go to him, but he can't come to me. (2 Samuel 12:23)

David's very human outpouring of emotion was a great comfort when our young son was sick and near death. First, David's story shows the confidence and power forgiveness brings. Guilty thoughts could have kept David from boldly approaching God, though he had confessed, repented, and found forgiveness for his sin. Instead David took God at His word. He confidently approached the Father as a forgiven man, without guilt. David's example became a beacon of hope when I struggled with guilt. His bold trust gave me confidence to approach God.

Second, David's actions showed that God wants parents to advocate for their children through prayer. It's a job God expected me to take seriously.

Third, the answer to David's prayer shows that healing is not God's only right response to prayer. God could have answered our prayers by taking our son and making him whole in the next life instead of this one.

Fourth, David's behavior after his son's death—self-care, worship, and eating—gave me permission to continue living and caring for my own needs even when our son was deathly ill. I prayed for strength and permission to live if Allen died.

Finally and most importantly, this passage says that if my son died, God would take him home. David's words, "I can go to him, but he can't come to me," clearly show that children who die before they're able to choose or reject God are in His presence when their lives end.

Five Lessons from David's Grief Story

1. God's forgiveness allows us to approach Him with boldness.
2. God wants parents to be prayer advocates for their children.
3. God sometimes allows long sickness or even death.
4. God gives us permission to continue living after the death of a child.
5. God takes little children to heaven where believing parents will see them again one day.

God the Father: The day Christ died on the cross is the darkest day in human history. The accounts of the crucifixion revolve around the horrific death of an innocent man, Jesus the Son of God, as they should. But His parents also hover nearby in the accounts. His mother, Mary, waits at the foot of the cross. God, His Father, watches from heaven. Here's how Luke describes the Father's response to Jesus' death:

> By now it was noon. The whole earth became dark, the darkness lasting three hours—a total blackout. The Temple curtain split right down the middle. Jesus called loudly, "Father, I place my life in your hands!" Then he breathed his last. (Luke 23:44–46)

The Father's grief was so great that the sun grew dark, His emotions so raw that He ripped the Temple curtain down the middle.

When the loss of your child sucks the light out of your world and you feel torn in two, look to your Father. He knows your grief. He bears your sorrow. His tears can heal your heart. Above all, cling to this truth. God had a good purpose for His Child's life and death. He has a purpose for your child, too. Cling to the hope of Christ found in Paul's words: "He who did not spare His own Son, but delivered Him over for us all, how will He not also with Him freely give us all things?" (Romans 8:32 NASB).

Faith in the Midst of Grief

During interviews for this book, I asked parents what tools helped them process their grief and stay close to God. Some regretfully said they didn't have anything. Several mentioned books, which are listed as resources at the end of this chapter. A few paused, and then mentioned some Bible verses. Two parents, DeAnn and Brittany, responded quickly and emphatically, saying, "I used the Bible."

Brittany adds, "It boiled down to a personal relationship with God, to prayer. We can talk to Him. I can't imagine going through what we did without Him."

Following Brittany's lead, you can use the Bible as a tool for expressing your grief. The prayer guide "Thirty Prayers for Grieving Families" in appendix A contains thirty verses you can use to cry out to God from the depths of your sorrow. By speaking God's words back to Him, you join the host of faithful, hurting saints who learned to stand on the promises in His Word when all else was lost.

DeAnn explains how she used the Bible when her son was dying: "I didn't want my feelings clouded by others' stories and conclusions. So I dug into the Bible to see what would speak to me. I carried a Gideon Bible with me everywhere and wrote verses on little sheets of paper. Later I transferred the verses into the journal that I kept and dated, so I could look back and see where God was faithful."

Appendix B also includes a list of verses that spoke to DeAnn through her grief. You may want to follow DeAnn's example and keep your own journal. Use it to jot down your questions for God, record verses to cling to when all seems dark, and note moments when God shows up.

Purpose in the Midst of Grief

The parents in this book who have lost children express two certainties. They believe God had a purpose for their children's lives, whether or not He has revealed it, and they believe that the rest of their lives will be a constant unwrapping of that purpose as God uses their experiences to change them and uses them to change the world.

Ethan's short life impacted his immediate family and the medical community. Ethan was one week old when he died of a massive brain bleed. Tests later revealed a rare genetic bleeding disorder. When Ethan's sister was born a year later, a blood test showed Annika has the same disorder. Ethan's mom, Tiffany, says, "She is alive because of Ethan." Her medical treatment is an ongoing experiment, with implications for the bleeding disorder community around the world.

Don and Victoria had never heard of Trisomy 18 before their son Isaac was born in 2001. Since then, Victoria has become an expert on the condition that occurs in one of every 3,000 live births. In 2003, she and Don founded the Trisomy 18 Foundation. At the foundation's website, www.trisomy18.org, Victoria says, "Every child's life, no matter how fragile their life or brief their days, forever changes our world." Her words are true. The nationally recognized Trisomy 18 Foundation, created in memory of their son who lived only eleven days, has served over 30,000 mothers, fathers, grandparents, and family supporters. God had a life-changing purpose for Isaac's short life.

Kurt and Joy's son Sam was born with a congenital heart condition. He spent his whole life, seventy-two days, in Mayo Clinic's Cardiac Intensive Care Unit (CICU), which cares for all heart patients, newborn to ninety. Joy explains, "The heart care they receive in

CICU is excellent, but the unit isn't set up to meet the special needs of newborns like NICU is."

During Sam's hospital stay, Kurt and Joy adapted some NICU techniques to sooth and calm their little boy. After he died, they used Sam's memorial money to create Snuggles from Sam, a comfort bag ministry for families of babies in CICUs. The custom-made bags contain a stuffed animal toy that plays soothing white noise for babies, an infant wrap with openings for medical tubes, an incubator-sized fleece blanket, a lullaby CD, a gas card, a devotional book for parents, and a card about their ministry.

"We thought about the ministry before Sam's death," Joy remembers, "but afterward, we really wanted to do it to draw people to God. He got us through this. I don't know how parents do it without Him."

Hope in the Midst of Grief

God had great purposes for the lives of Ethan, Isaac, and Sam. He has a great purpose for your child's life and for your grief, even if you can't yet discern it. In *Holding onto Hope*, Nancy Guthrie explains how she learned wait until God chose to reveal His purposes, if He ever chose to reveal them: "Instead of demanding an answer, you decide to trust him, recognizing that your circumstances provide an unparalleled opportunity to glorify God just by your trust in his unseen purpose."

You can trust God with your grief. You can trust Him with your pain. You can trust Him with your loss because He is a Father who understands the pain of a world gone dark and a heart torn in two. He is the Father who has lost a Son. He is the God of grief and of purpose. He is the God you can trust.

Oh God, why did my child have to die? How can I bear such a loss? How did you bear the loss of your Son? Hold me close, Father. Cry with me. Then dry my tears so I can see beyond them to your purpose in this deep sorrow.

How is my grief like that of the biblical parents mentioned in this chapter? What can I learn from their grief? How will I cry out to God and ask my questions? How did the Father and the Son respond to death? How will I respond?

Take Time to Reflect

Resources

Books

- Nancy Guthrie, *Holding onto Hope: A Pathway Through Suffering to the Heart of God* (Tyndale, 2006).
- Nancy Guthrie, *Jesus Speaks Into Your Sorrow* (Tyndale, 2009).
- Nancy Guthrie, *The One Year Book of Hope* (Tyndale, 2005).
- Jerry Sittser, *A Grace Disguised: How the Soul Grows through Loss* (Zondervan, 2004).
- Joni Eareckson Tada, *Glorious Intruder: God's Presence in Life's Chaos* (Multnomah, 1989).

Online Resources

- Trisomy 18 Foundation: www.trisomy18.org
- Information about Snuggles from Sam can be found at www.differentdream.com by typing "Snuggles from Sam" in the search box.

Raising a Survivor

From Fragile to Fearless

21

Fearless in Body

There has never been the slightest doubt in my
mind that the God who started this great work in
you would keep at it and bring it to a flourishing finish on the very day Christ Jesus appears.

Philippians 1:6

When we ask God to make people whole, we're
thinking of how we see "whole." I think there's more
beauty in the broken things. Brokenness gives kids
tender hearts.

Laurie, mother of two girls with physical,
mental, and developmental needs

Gary and Laurie adopted Neveah and Angelina after they became
their eighth foster care placement. Over time, the girls were
diagnosed with a string of disorders: bipolar, ADHD, and a variety
of developmental and physical delays. During their first four years as
a family, Laurie read books and attended parenting classes to manage

the chaos caused by the adoption. Once Laurie joined a local support group, she gained confidence and learned more creative parenting and self-care skills. In addition to parenting four kids (two biological daughters, Rebecca and Anna, are now part of the family), Laurie is a professional life coach, helping women develop family relationships and thrive in the midst of stress.

Becoming fearless survivors: Neveah, nine, and Angelina, eight

Dean and Maureen's third child, Jennifer, surprised them by arriving twelve weeks early. After three months in NICU, punctuated with surgeries and setbacks due to underdeveloped lungs, a hole in her heart, and hydrocephalus, they brought Jennifer home on her due date. More surgeries over several years corrected her health issues. She attended special classes in the public school and moved to a residential facility on her eighteenth birthday. Jennifer now lives in a group home with several friends, works thirty hours a week, and regularly invites friends to church. Her pastor says, "Jennifer is the best evangelist we've ever had."

Living a full and fearless life: Jennifer, thirty-two

The day after Sydney was born, Jeff and Shelby noticed an odd indentation in their daughter's spine. An ultrasound revealed no anomalies, but her parents were skeptical. An MRI done when Sydney was fifteen months old revealed she had a tethered spinal cord, an extra vertebra, and fatty tissue deposits. Surgery corrected her physical problems, but poor preparation for the MRI and a three-day stay in a pediatric intensive care unit at eighteen months left emotional scars. Sydney later developed a separation anxiety so severe that she has to be homeschooled. Her parents hope that treatment for anxiety and post-traumatic stress disorder (PTSD) will allow her to return to school soon.

Overcoming and surviving fear: Sydney, eight

Andrew and Ellen were twenty-six when their second child, Nichole, was born with Down syndrome. Once they discovered the beauty of parenting both Ellie, their typical daughter, and Nichole, they chose to adopt a child with special needs. Nina was three when Andrew and Ellen rescued her from possible death in a Ukrainian orphanage. Andrew and Ellen treat all three of their daughters as capable. They celebrate passionately when challenges are overcome. Ellen says, "So many kids with special needs aren't celebrated enough."

Celebrating, surviving, and thriving: Nina, five, and Nichole, four

From Fragile to Fearless

Parents don't come with a delete button to erase their recollections of the early days of raising a child with special needs. Close your eyes, and the memories rush in. Your fragile newborn, more tubes and wires than flesh, struggling to live. Your child fighting cancer, nauseated by chemo treatments. Your teenager, learning to walk and talk and control his bowels after surviving a bad car accident.

For many parents, those memories are liberating reminders of the progress made over the years. But for some parents, the memories can become a trap. The mind-set that serves parents well during a crisis can evolve into unhealthy everyday parenting habits that keep children with special needs from living fully and fearlessly. Therefore when a child's condition stabilizes, parents must adjust to everyday childrearing so that the child is equipped to survive as a fearless adult.

The remainder of this book deals with challenges unique to families of survivors with special needs. This chapter talks about how to avoid an unhealthy mind-set and create a healthy one. The next chapter examines mental health concerns common to children with special needs. Chapter 23 is about making financial and legal plans for the future. The final chapter discusses ways for parents to pass on their faith to their children. Let's start by checking out some common parent traps that can lead to an unhealthy mind-set.

Recognizing and Resisting Parent Traps

Our son usually calls us on the weekends. During those calls, if he coughs or sounds the least bit congested, my mind goes into overdrive. *Is he getting bronchitis? Will it turn into pneumonia? He needs to see a doctor. He needs to sleep elevated. Where's the vaporizer?*

Never mind that Allen's last surgery was in 1997, and he's been healthy ever since. Never mind that he graduated from high school in 2001. Never mind that he got married in 2010. Never mind that my thoughts are completely irrational. I'm his mama, he's my man cub, and I'm gonna save my little critter.

Snap. Caught in a parent trap. Again.

Yes, I'm still a sucker for parent traps. But over the years I've learned to recognize and resist the following unhealthy ones.

Defining a Child by a Condition or Disease: How do you introduce or describe your child to others? Do you mention your child's condition first, or do say he's an eight-year-old kid who loves football, Spiderman, and computers, and then mention special needs? If you put the condition or disease first or mention it exclusively, you're allowing it to define your child. That's not healthy. It limits your child and your perception of your child, as well as the perceptions of others. How can a child reach his full potential if you and others define him by only his needs?

Defining Yourself as a Caregiver: Closely related to defining a child by his or her condition is defining yourself as a caregiver. Allowing that one role to define you is unhealthy. Who will you be when your child doesn't need your care? Where will you find worth if you're no longer able to be a caregiver?

Overprotecting a Survivor: After years of protecting a child from germs, teasing, stares, pity, and a host of other dangers, it is hard to let a child enter the big, bad world. For your child's sake, you need to stifle the urge to overprotect. You must gradually release your child while you're available to give advice and help problem solve. Otherwise your child won't be prepared for the day when you're not around.

Denying Sexuality: If your child has significant developmental delays, it might be tempting to pretend puberty will never happen. But it will, and sexuality issues must be addressed before puberty to protect your child's safety and health. If you don't know where to start, talk to a health care worker, teacher, or support group about resources. Marsh Media's website, www.marshmedia.com, is an excellent resource. At the site, you can download a free, informative document about sex education for students with special needs.

Dwelling on What Might Have Been: While it's healthy for parents to acknowledge and grieve for lost dreams, excessive and exclusive focus on who your child might have been is a dangerous practice. That kind of tunnel vision won't allow you to enjoy the wonderful person your child is now. Do you want to fall into that trap and lose both the child you dreamed of having *and* the child you do have?

The list of parent traps could go on and on, but maybe you're getting the idea. Any mind-set that limits a child's future is a trap to avoid.

Five Parent Traps to Avoid

1. Defining a child by a disease or condition.
2. Defining yourself exclusively as a caregiver.
3. Overprotecting a child.
4. Denying a child's maturation and sexuality.
5. Dwelling on what might have been.

Creating a Healthy Mindset

Let's look at techniques several parents use to steer clear of parent traps and build a healthy mind-set.

Take Care of Yourself: Laurie learned to practice self-care after she and her husband adopted two daughters who have bipolar disorders as well as physical and developmental delays. At first, she tried to do everything on her own. Life descended into chaos, and she had no time for herself. Finally, she and her husband took action. "We've cut expenses so we could hire an assistant. We applied for and received special adoption funds to pay for child care. Now I can carve out time for myself so I can get away and relax." Today she even has time to blog and share self-care and stress management tips at www .lauriewallin.com.

Time for yourself does more than ease stress. It allows you to develop roles beyond those of parent and caregiver. You can develop hobbies, participate in activities you enjoy, and nurture friendships. When your role as your child's primary caregiver ends or changes, you'll handle the transition better because you've cultivated new roles to replace old ones.

Teach Your Child How to Cope: Alison's son, Lars, was diagnosed with Asperger's syndrome in elementary school. Because Lars wanted to go to college, Alison started teaching him coping and organizational strategies. Over and over she told him, "The rest of the world won't change for you. You have to cope with the world."

She admits she was a wreck his freshman year of college. He called three or four times a week, asking what to do. Over time, he learned to cope. He doesn't have close friends, but Alison says that's okay. "He knows he has a large extended family. He knows we are here for him."

Keep in Mind What's Best for Your Child: Marla was born in the early 1970s, when parents of children with Down syndrome were advised to place them in an institution. Thanks to a family doctor who told Marvin and Doris, "Your daughter needs you," they decided to raise Marla at home. Their daughter was a trailblazer throughout her childhood, entering public school one year before the federal Individuals with Disabilities Act (IDEA) mandated special education for all children. When she saw her siblings graduate from high school and go to college, she said she wanted to move away from home after high school too. So her parents visited several residential facilities until they found the one best suited to her needs. "When making decisions, we try to keep in mind what's best for her," Doris says. "We're still very involved in her life."

Rich and Sharon's son, Tim, requires intense physical care because of severe cerebral palsy. They knew they would not be able to meet his care needs as they grew older. After high school, Tim toured several facilities with his parents and moved into a residential center for adults with disabilities. Sharon says, "It's okay to put an adult child in residential care. He needed it. We needed it, and the transition is easier for a younger person."

Only you can make the right decision for your child's future as an adult. Consider all of your options as your child approaches adulthood, and then choose the best one. Base your decisions on what is best for your child's present and future.

Collect Appreciative People: Pete and Chelsea are parents of two kids with special needs. Justus has autism and bipolar disorder. Noelle lives with Asperger's syndrome. Both are old enough to realize they are different from other kids, so their parents work hard to help them develop healthy attitudes. Chelsea describes two strategies they use. First, they surround themselves and their children with people who appreciate Justus and Noelle for who they are and who share similar interests. Their acceptance creates a support group for their entire family.

Second, they encourage their children to bravely be who they are. A quote from Dr. Seuss is popular at their house: "Be who you are and say what you feel because those who mind don't matter and those who matter don't mind."

Being surrounded by people who appreciate you and your kids and have similar interests sounds downright healthy, doesn't it? Can you think of who you want in your collection of appreciative people?

> ## Four Ways to Create a Healthy Mind-set
>
> 1. Take care of yourself.
> 2. Teach your child to cope.
> 3. Keep in mind what's best for your child.
> 4. Collect appreciative people.

Growing Up Is Normal

Growing up is a normal part of life. Our job as parents is to prepare our children for adult life and for the time when we leave this earth. Whether our kids develop typically or have special needs, we must teach them to be as independent as possible. God wants us to avoid parent traps so we can pass a healthy mind-set on to our kids. A healthy mind-set is the first component necessary for parents who want to raise fearless survivors. Next let's explore a second component: meeting the mental health issues of kids with special needs.

Dear Father, thank you for the privilege of raising my child. It would be so easy to fall into the old thought patterns I developed when my child was young and life was tenuous. Help me create a new, healthier attitude so my child can become a true, independent survivor.

What parent traps do I fall into? How will they harm my child? What do I need to change to better meet my child's needs? What can I do to foster greater independence in my child?

Take Time to Reflect

Resources

Special Needs Blogs

- Laurie Wallin, Living Power: www.lauriewallin.com
- Love That Max: www.lovethatmax.com
- 5 Minutes for Special Needs: www.5minutesforspecialneeds.com
- Different Dream: www.DifferentDream.com
- Support for Special Needs: www.supportforspecialneeds.com
- Comfort in the Midst of Chaos: www.comfortinthemidstofchaos.blogspot.com
- Wrestling with an Angel: www.sheepdogger.blogspot.com

Parenting Blog

- Because I Said So: www.dawnmeehan.com

Special Needs Parenting Resources

- Foster W. Cline and Lisa Greene, *Parenting Children with Health Issues: Essential Tools, Tips, and Tactics for Raising Kids with Chronic Illness, Medical Conditions, and Special Healthcare Needs* (Love and Logic Press, 2007).
- Marsh Media: www.marshmedia.com/pages/special.cfm
- Mary Wrobel, *Taking Care of Yourself: A Hygiene, Puberty, and Personal Curriculum for Young People with Autism* (Future Horizons, 2003).

22

Fearless in Mind

> For God did not give us a spirit of timidity, but a
> spirit of power, of love and of self-discipline.
>
> 2 Timothy 1:7 (NIV)
>
> It makes me sad that Sydney hasn't had a carefree
> childhood. I'm amazed when people don't under-
> stand post-traumatic stress disorder.
>
> Shelby, mom of Sydney,
> who developed post-traumatic
> stress disorder after an
> MRI at eighteen months

We saw our son for the first time in NICU after the surgery that connected his esophagus to his stomach. His tiny torso bristled with wires held in place by patches. An angry red scar stretched from under his arm to his backbone. Monitors lined the wall. Bags hung from an IV pole, and tubes snaked from it into his motionless body.

I didn't cry until I saw the pain lines etched in the baby soft skin around Allen's tiny mouth.

"Will this affect him emotionally?" we asked the nurse.

"Don't worry," she assured us. "A baby's nerves aren't as developed as adults, so they don't feel pain like we do. They don't even need pain medication. He won't remember a thing."

Still the expression on Allen's face worried my husband and me. Our baby *looked* like he was in pain. Throughout his stay in NICU and before subsequent invasive medical procedures and surgery, we asked doctor after doctor and nurse after nurse the same question: "How will this affect him emotionally?" Year after year, surgery after surgery, the answer never varied: "He'll be fine. Babies don't feel pain like we do. He won't remember a thing."

For a while, once Allen's physical health was restored, we believed what we'd been told. He was a good student, had lots of friends, and his teachers loved him. But every now and then, when he felt physically trapped or restrained, he literally bit and fought like a caged animal.

We thought his reactions were normal until adolescence, when he became increasingly impulsive. He made plans and set goals, but rarely carried through. In one day, he would morph from charming to manipulative to angry to obstinate to infantile and back again. After his junior year of high school, he ran away for the first time. Over the next several years, he developed a pattern of running from stressful situations. Finally, after eight years away from home, he called and said, "I need to figure out what's wrong with me. I can't hold a job. I can't get married. I can't have a family. Will you help me?"

With those words, God set a series of events into motion. Two days after the call, we had a name for Allen's condition—post-traumatic stress disorder (PTSD), caused by the invasive medical procedures he wasn't supposed to remember. A week later, he began outpatient treatment at an innovative trauma clinic. After five days of intensive therapy, he knew how to cope with what he'd experienced as a young child.

Mental health treatment changed Allen's life. He is a now a reliable, trusted employee. He makes plans and set goals. He and his wife look forward to starting a family. We are grateful for both of his healings—the surgeries that saved his life when he was a child and the therapy that restored his life to wholeness and peace.

Before Allen's treatment, we believed mental illnesses existed, but because mental illnesses can't be seen or touched, like a broken leg or a swollen appendix, treatment seemed like a shot in the dark. If a correct diagnosis was made, maybe a therapist could help a patient manage mental illness. But a cure? Impossible.

Needless to say, our thinking changed after Allen's experience. We now know that many mental illnesses can be diagnosed with accuracy. And as is true of physical illnesses, some mental illnesses can be successfully treated and some can't.

Parents who have mental health concerns about their kids must advocate as passionately and boldly as they do for physical health concerns. To do so, parents must be aware of symptoms of mental illness and available treatments. Because one chapter can't touch on every childhood mental illness, we'll concentrate on PTSD. Why? Because kids with special needs have a high risk of developing it.

What Is PTSD?

The Minnesota Association for Children's Mental Health says, "Children who are involved in or witness to a traumatic event that involved intense fear, helplessness, or horror are at risk for developing post-traumatic stress disorder." They list several events considered traumatic for children: serious accidents, abuse, natural disasters, or severe injury. Absent from the list are invasive pediatric medical treatments and procedures, but they certainly match the descriptors of "intense fear, helplessness, and horror."

245

Children usually begin exhibiting symptoms of PTSD within three months of the traumatic event, though in some cases the symptoms don't surface until years later. In children, the symptoms may include flashbacks, sleeping difficulties, and repetitive play referring to the event or reenactment. According to the *Diagnostic and Statistical Manual of Mental Disorders* (DSM), a diagnosis of PTSD is made only when the symptoms persist for more than a month. For a diagnosis to be made, the condition must also significantly impair the patient's ability to function effectively.

Not all children who have invasive medical treatment develop PTSD. Dr. Linda Gantt, a therapist at Intensive Trauma Therapy in Morgantown, West Virginia, identified four risk factors that increase the likelihood it will develop:

1. PTSD is more likely to occur in emergency situations than in scheduled situations when there's time to prepare the child beforehand. PTSD is less likely if the preparation is age-appropriate.

2. A patient's inability to go under or "partial awakening" during the procedure increases the likelihood of PTSD. The type of anesthetic should be selected based on the procedure and age of the patient.

3. The younger the patient, the greater the risk. Nonverbal children, birth to age three, are at greatest risk.

4. Children who have experienced previous significant trauma (sexual abuse, physical abuse, life-threatening situations) are more likely to develop PTSD after medical treatment.

How Is PTSD Treated?

If your child had a broken leg or an ear infection, you would seek immediate treatment. If your child's symptoms of PTSD persist more than three months, it's time to seek treatment, too. Finding a qualified practitioner trained in the treatment of PTSD often

Symptoms of PTSD in Children

- Flashbacks, nightmares, or repetitive play referencing the event
- Emotional distress when reminded of the event
- Physical reactions when reminded of the event, including headache, stomachache, dizziness
- Inability to fall or stay asleep
- Fear or avoidance of certain places, things, or conversations that remind them of the event
- Denial of the event or inability to recall an important aspect of it
- A foreshortened sense of the future
- Difficulty concentrating
- Startle easily
- Self-destructive behavior, irritability, and impulsiveness
- Depression and overwhelming sadness or hopelessness

Adapted from the Minnesota Association for Mental Health's "Children's Mental Health Fact Sheet for the Classroom: Post-Traumatic Stress Disorder."

requires persistence, as the field and training are relatively new. Your pediatrician may be able to refer you to a pediatric therapist or counselor. A child life specialist or social worker at the nearest children's hospital may also have recommendations. Check local government resources, including your county, as some counties have extensive mental health programs to assist not only the child but also parents.

Several treatments are available. Eye Movement Desensitization and Reprocessing (EMDR) is an effective and widespread treatment that may be available in your area. Cognitive-Behavioral Therapy (CBT) and play therapy are also widely used. More information about the intensive treatment our son received can be found at www .traumatherapy.us.

How Can PTSD Be Prevented?

Preventative measures can greatly reduce your child's risk of developing PTSD. If a child life specialist had prepared Sydney for her MRI when she was fifteen months old, her fear of uniforms and masks, her strange nightmares, and her severe separation anxiety might have been avoided. (A discussion of the role of child life specialists in preventing trauma can be found in chapter 6.) Of course, in the case of an emergency, there's no time for preventative measures. Even so, children who work with a therapist or child life specialist soon after the surgery or procedure are far less likely to develop PTSD.

> **Effective PTSD Treatment Methods**
> - Eye Movement Desensitization and Reprocessing (EMDR)
> - Cognitive-Behavioral Therapy (CBT)
> - Intensive Trauma Therapy (ITT)

If a hospital does not have child life specialists, you will have to help your child yourself. In *Trauma-Proofing Your Kids*, authors Peter Levine and Maggie Kline teach parents to administer "first aid for trauma prevention." Parents can use the step-by-step instructions for a series of exercises soon after the traumatic event. Later, if PTSD symptoms develop and persist, parents should seek professional help.

What Are Other Causes of PTSD?

Not all PTSD in kids with special needs is related to medical intervention. Other causes include abuse of any kind, neglect, natural disasters, accidents, divorce, the death of a loved one, moving, or adoption. Because many parents adopt children with special needs, its link to PTSD deserves our attention.

Andy and Ellen adopted three-year-old Nina from the Ukraine. Resources and staff members are stretched thin at orphanages in that country, which often leads to neglect. Therefore, Nina's new parents watched their daughter closely for signs of trauma. One day during playtime, Nina used a belt to tie down her doll in the crib. She told the doll she had been "naughty." Since then, her parents have been helping her process what happened at the orphanage. Nina hasn't exhibited other symptoms of PTSD, but Andy and Ellen continue to monitor her behavior carefully.

Not all adopted children develop PTSD, but even those adopted as newborns by loving parents are at higher risk than the general population, as Alice and Nichole's story demonstrates. Alice adopted Nichole at birth. From day one, Nichole was anxious whenever Alice was gone. Her separation anxiety increased through her preschool years. Since age five, she has received counseling and drug therapy for anxiety disorder, bipolar disorder, and attention deficit hyperactive disorder (ADHD), all with limited success. PTSD therapy at age fourteen resulted in significant improvement, though Nichole still struggles in many areas.

Two factors increase the risk of PTSD and other mental illnesses in children who are adopted: the age of a child at adoption and severity of abuse or neglect experienced before adoption. Depending on experiences, genetic makeup, and resilience, these children may also be susceptible to mental illnesses such as reactive attachment disorder (RAD), oppositional defiant disorder (ODD), attention deficit disorder (ADD), ADHD, and bipolar disorder.

Adoptive families of kids with these diagnoses need professional guidance, a strong, committed support system, and a vast supply of resources to weather the storms of parenting. Jayne Schooler's book *Wounded Children, Healing Homes: How Traumatized*

Children Impact Adoptive and Foster Families is a storehouse of resources and realistic encouragement for parents raising children scarred by trauma.

Twenty-Six Years?

Most medical practitioners no longer deny the traumatizing effects of invasive medical procedures on children. Diagnosis and treatment of PTSD and mental illnesses has improved greatly since our son's birth in 1982. He was twenty-six before his PTSD was diagnosed and treated. After he completed therapy, he looked at me and said, "Mom, for the first time in my life I'm not looking over my shoulder waiting for someone to take me into surgery again."

My heart sank at his words. Had my baby really lived with constant fear for twenty-six years?

Twenty-six years. A long time to wait, but it couldn't be helped. The resources he needed didn't exist in the 1980s. But they do exist today. If you suspect your child has a mental illness, pursue treatment. Your child can have a carefree childhood. What a wonderful gift to give! What a difference it could make in your child's life!

Dear God, thank you for restoring my child's physical health. My desire is to help my child be mentally healthy, too. Don't let me deny symptoms of mental illness. Instead, give me eyes to recognize them and the will to pursue treatment. Show me what to do to make my child whole again.

Has my child experienced traumatic events? Is my child exhibiting symptoms of PTSD or another mental illness? What diagnostic and treatment facilities are available in our area? How can I contact them?

Take Time to Reflect

Resources

Books

- Peter A. Levine and Maggie Kline, *Trauma Through a Child's Eyes* (North Atlantic Books, 2006).
- Peter A. Levine and Maggie Kline, *Trauma-Proofing Your Kids* (North Atlantic Books, 2008).
- Jayne Schooler, *Wounded Children, Healing Homes: How Traumatized Children Impact Adoptive and Foster Families* (NavPress, 2010).

Mental Health Organizations

- Intensive Trauma Therapy Institute: www.traumatherapy.us
- National Child Traumatic Stress Network (NCTSN): www.nctsnet.org. Go to the website and click on the "Understanding Child Traumatic Stress" button to access several downloadable publications. For information specific to children who are deaf or have developmental delays, click "Topics" in the left column, and then "Special Populations and Trauma."
- Minnesota Association for Children's Mental Health: www.macmh.org. Go to the website and type "PTSD" in the search box. When the new page pops up, click on "Children's Mental Health Fact Sheets." You can download fact sheets on fifteen mental illnesses including PTSD, RAD, eating disorders, and ADD.
- Children's Hospital of Philadelphia: www.aftertheinjury.org

23

Fearless about the Future

Religion that God our Father accepts as pure and
faultless is this: to look after orphans and widows in
their distress . . .

James 1:27 (NIV)

We had to think about what happens if Jennifer out-
lives us. Parents have to realize the truth. If you die,
what will your child have?

Dean, father of Jennifer,
who is now a young woman

Before Allen was born, the thought that we could have a child
with special needs rarely occurred to us. Four years after his birth,
when we considered expanding our family again, the "what ifs"
haunted us. What if our next child had medical issues too? What if
we had twins—they ran in both of our families—and they were born
prematurely? What if a new baby had developmental delays in addition to physical challenges?

Because of my experiences with a disabled father, my what ifs projected far into the future. What if our next child had special needs that required a lifetime of care? What if we died before our child? Who would provide care then? We couldn't expect Allen to take that on, could we? What if the only option was a residential facility? Who would pay for that?

My what ifs evaporated when our daughter was born with a fully functioning body, a sound mind, and an easy disposition. Both our children, it seemed, would follow the path of most kids. They would become independent adults and make their way in the world.

Independent adulthood is not a realistic expectation for all children. Even so, parents can financially equip their children to be as independent as possible. To accomplish this, parents should engage in sound, long-term financial and legal planning to provide for their child's needs throughout his or her adult life.

In this chapter, you'll learn how to start your financial planning and what basic legal documents should be in place. You'll also learn about resources to help you locate reputable financial planners and lawyers who specialize in the special needs field.

Why Plan for the Future?

Jeff Rupp is a special needs financial advisor in Florida. During free, introductory financial planning seminars for parents of kids with special needs, he reviews the following statistics:

- Nine out of ten parents have no financial and estate plan in place for their children with special needs.
- Seventy-five percent of the plans in place are faulty, so children are in danger of losing government assistance monies.
- Three to five percent of parents have a proper plan in place for their children with special needs.

These statistics are disturbing because when kids with special needs turn eighteen, they become legal adults, regardless of intellectual ability or development, and legal adults receiving government assistance lose their eligibility if they have more than two thousand dollars in assets. Without a good plan in place, children who receive Social Security Insurance (SSI), Medicaid, and Medicaid waiver programs as minors will lose their benefits at age eighteen if the government finds they have two thousand or more dollars in their names.

If parents received faulty financial advice and saved money in their child's name instead of putting it in a special needs trust, their child loses all government benefits on his or her eighteenth birthday. Or if the parents die without a proper estate plan and the adult child inherits the estate, benefits are revoked. Not only that, but the government will confiscate inherited assets to compensate for previous benefits paid. The surviving adult child becomes penniless immediately or when the remaining money runs out. Either way, the adult with special needs becomes a ward of the state.

Who Should Be on the Planning Team?

To avoid these repercussions, parents should form a special needs planning team. Who should be on it? Rupp suggests parents enlist at least a financial planner, an attorney, and an accountant with training in special needs.

According to Erica Ferranti, a trust and estates lawyer with Armor Trust Attorneys in Raleigh, North Carolina, parents should start planning when their children are young because "there is always a risk that something will happen to both parents while the child is a minor, and if they haven't done any planning, that can be a devastating situation."

How can parents locate qualified professionals? On the next page are several suggestions for building your team. Be aware that special needs trust laws vary from state to state, as do specialized certification for lawyers and financial planners. So be sure to search for professionals who have experience in your state.

How to Build a Special Needs Planning Team

- In an Internet search engine, type the name of your state followed by "special needs trust attorney." Do the same with "special needs financial planning" and "special needs accountant." Then search again, substituting "disability" for "special needs."
- Visit the Special Needs Alliance website (www .specialneedsalliance.com) to locate a special needs attorney in your state.
- Contact the nearest ARC chapter (see the chapter locator at www.thearc.org) to ask for recommendations.
- Ask other parents for recommendations.

What role will each member of the team play? The attorney assists with writing a will, the special needs trust, and other legal documents. The financial advisor helps with savings plans and life insurance concerns. The accountant does the budgeting and provides assistance regarding tax law.

Ferranti suggests finding an attorney who does special needs legal work on a regular basis. "Ask how often the attorney drafts special needs trusts. An attorney who has experience with special needs trusts will most likely know which local trust companies or banks to recommend," she says. "Finally, trust your gut. If you leave the attorney's office and feel like you didn't get good answers to your questions, you probably need to find a different lawyer." Once you apply the same criteria to the selection of a qualified financial planner and accountant, your team will be in place.

Before meeting with your lawyer and other members of the planning team, Ferranti suggests parents do some preplanning:

1. Create a list of your assets, how they are titled, and their approximate values. The list should include real estate, vehicles, life insurance, retirement benefits and plans, and investment accounts.
2. Think about who you want to name as executor, durable power of attorney, and health care power of attorney.
3. Consider your child's future needs. Is your child likely to qualify for government benefits in the future if he doesn't already? Or will you be self-funding your child's future care?

When you're done with the preplanning, you're ready to meet with the professional team.

What Legal Documents Should Be in Place?

Both Rupp and Ferranti suggest parents put several legal documents in place: a last will and testament, a durable power of attorney, a health care power of attorney (with a HIPAA release for themselves), and a trust for their child.

Special Circumstances to Consider

- If the child is a minor, parents need only a Special Needs Trust and Will that designates a guardian for the minor child.
- If the child is eighteen or older and competent, the child should execute a Durable Power of Attorney and a Health Care Power of Attorney with HIPPA Release.
- If the child is eighteen or older and not competent, parents need to be appointed as legal guardians so they can manage the child's finances and make health care decisions.

The type of trust created will vary, depending on your child's circumstances and state law, though usually a special needs trust is the best choice. In the trust, you appoint trustees to manage your child's finances after you are gone. A good trustee for a special needs trust can be a trust company, a banker, a financial advisor, or an attorney. Family members and friends may also be options depending on the type of trust you choose. The sidebar on the previous page explains circumstances to consider while creating the trust.

If you are confused by what you are reading, remember that's why you are working with professionals in the field of special needs. What's confusing to you is normal, everyday practice for them.

How to Further Protect Your Child

With the proper legal and financial framework in place, you can breathe a sigh of relief about the monetary provisions for your child's future. But Ferranti says it's also important to plan for a child's emotional and social welfare. She wants parents to be sure their child has a network of caring people who can step in when a parent dies—people who will make sure the child doesn't end up isolated and without a support network.

Ferranti suggests parents write a Letter of Intent. In it they "tell future caregivers and trustees about the child's needs, desires, and goals. This is often a very personal document and covers details about a child's life that don't belong in the trust document, but can be very helpful in the future administration of the trust."

Finally, she advises parents to obtain disability and long-term care insurance for themselves. Otherwise, when they become disabled or elderly, their care needs could use up all the assets they were planning to use to fund their child's trust.

How to Begin

Does the financial and legal process seem daunting? Not to worry. Break it down into smaller, less intimidating tasks. Start by asking

God to guide you to people with professional expertise and a passion for kids with special needs. Then educate yourself using the resources at the end of the chapter. Move forward one step at a time, and trust God to enable you to practice the pure and faultless faith He calls us to in James 1:27, "to look after orphans and widows in their distress."

Dear Giver of all gifts, you are the God who has provided all we needed to care for and raise our children. You are the God who will provide all our children need when we are no longer here. Show us how to steward our resources and be an instrument of your provision throughout our child's future.

What legal documents do we already have in place for our children? What financial planning have we already done? What is our next step in preparing for their futures? What professionals can help us? Which friends and family members do we want to be part of our child's support network when we are gone?

Take Time to Reflect

Resources

Special Needs Organizations

- The ARC: www.thearc.org
- Special Needs Alliance: www.specialneedsalliance.com

- Contact information for each state's Protection and Advocacy Agencies can be found at: http://www.autismspeaks.org/docs /family_services_docs/State_PA_Agencies.pdf

Special Needs Financial Planning Resources

- Goodwin Proctor's Guide is a twenty page document with legal information for families of children with autism. Much of it applies to other special needs. Go to www.autismspeaks .org and pull down on the "Be Informed" tab. Then click on "Your Child's Rights."
- Many reputable life insurance companies have a special needs planning division. Learn more at their websites by typing "special needs planning" into the search box.
- Merrill Lynch and *Exceptional Parent* magazine offer an online special needs planning seminar and downloadable PDF transcripts of the sessions. Go to www.totalmerrill.com/Total Merrill/pages/SpecialNeedsFinancialServices.aspx, and then click on the "Merrill Lynch and *Exceptional Parent* Magazine Special Needs Planning Seminar" link.

24

Fearless in Spirit

I prayed for this child, and God gave me what I
asked for. And now I have dedicated him to God.
He's dedicated to God for life.

1 Samuel 1:27–28

I wish we had started praying with Kim sooner. We
underestimated her ability to access God.

Paul, father of an adult daughter,
Kim, who has autism

Before Allen's birth condition was diagnosed, I thought our newborn baby belonged to us. But as events unfolded rapidly, God revealed His truth. When we heard Allen would be life-flighted to Omaha, Nebraska, for surgery, Hiram took my hand. "Thank you, Father, for giving Allen to us," my usually quiet husband prayed. "He's yours, God, not ours. You loved him before we knew him, and he belongs to you. Be with him when we can't. Amen."

My heart ached for my son and tears still flowed freely, but Hiram's prayer was a great comfort. Allen had been given to us by God. By entrusting him to God, we acknowledged a truth I now hold dear: During their childhoods, my husband and I were our children's stewards, but Allen and Anne belonged to the God who gave them life and breath.

Putting that truth into practice was hard for me when Allen was young and his health was tenuous. I thought it would be easier when his health issues faded. Boy, was I wrong. Raising our little survivor came with its own set of challenges. Allen was a strong-willed child, a fact he made clear as a three-year-old. When his behavior warranted a time-out, he would sit on his chair and yell, "I want my own way! You need to give me my own way!"

During his adolescence, the convergence of Allen's strong will and the effects of his undiagnosed PTSD tested our endurance frequently. It was a challenge to parent in a way that consistently reflected Christ to our son and to trust that God was working in Allen's life when our efforts seemed fruitless.

To some extent, every believing parent faces those two challenges. For parents of kids with special needs, the challenges can have a different flavor. Kids with special needs have varied intellectual and physical abilities, as well as behaviors and mental health concerns, and there is no one-size-fits-all strategy for tackling the challenges. So in this chapter, you'll hear from parents of kids of different ages and abilities. They'll talk about how they try to reflect Christ to their kids and how they entrust their children's spiritual formation to God.

Adapting Church Activities

For too long, churches have not accommodated or been accessible to those with special needs. However, as was mentioned in chapter 15, many churches are now reaching out to people with special needs and their families. In addition to what was covered in that chapter, the experiences of these parents may give you more ideas about simple accommodations to suggest at your church.

In the 1980s Dean and Maureen's daughter, Jennifer, wanted to attend confirmation. The pastor of their small town church and his wife welcomed the eighth grader whose premature birth resulted in cerebral palsy, developmental delays, and a seizure disorder. One of Jennifer's greatest strengths is singing, though she can't read music. Her confirmation teachers capitalized on that strength. Rather than excusing her from the required memory verses, they let her put them to music and sing them. The immediate result? Jennifer was confirmed with her peers. The long-term result? Jennifer still has God's Word hidden as a song in her heart. Now an adult, Jennifer lives in a group home and works thirty hours a week. She's active in a church that welcomes people with special needs.

Paul learned a valuable lesson from Kim, his daughter, who has autism and is nonverbal. She frequently launched into irritating behaviors when Paul and his wife, Jill, did their morning devotions. They would tell her to stop, without much success. One day Paul realized praying for and with Kim was a better solution. "I wish Jill and I had done it earlier," he says. "We taught her to pray. We also read a Bible story with her daily."

Eventually they started a Sunday school class for Kim and other adults with developmental delays. They discovered that the people attending the class didn't know the Bible stories. To internalize the stories, they needed to do more than just sit and listen. So under the direction of Paul and Jill, they began acting out the stories.

Also during the Sunday school class, class members spoke about the sin patterns they faced in daily life. "Some class members tend to obsess on someone and have trouble forgiving," Paul explains. "So 'love your enemy' lessons apply to them. Some struggle with honesty, stubbornness, and willfulness. We talk about how to surrender their wills to God."

Paul and Jill's efforts are a reminder of the importance of sharing our faith with our children using creative methods to foster understanding. We can't allow their special needs to prevent them from knowing Jesus and applying His truths to their lives.

Praying for Your Survivor

As parents and believers, we want our children to come to new life in Christ, but we can't make them believe. Once our kids are mature enough to decide for themselves, God alone can bring them to faith. However, we are not reduced to wringing our hands while we wait for God to complete His work.

We can cultivate a loving relationship with our kids, so they see the compassion of Christ through us, no matter what choices they make. And we can pray for our children, in all circumstances, asking God to fulfill the promises of His Word in their lives. Use the following prayers and passages to gather ideas about how to pray for your child.

Ellen and her husband, Andrew, have three children. Ellie, their oldest daughter is typical, Nina has cerebral palsy, and Nichole has Down syndrome. Ellen says they ask God to bless all three girls in the same way. "Our prayer is for them to know and follow God, for Him to protect them all their lives, and that He will use them mightily."

During Chelsea's pregnancies, her husband, Pete, prayed that their children would have good hearts. After Justus was diagnosed with autism as a toddler and Noelle was diagnosed with Asperger's a few years later, Chelsea began praying a verse from 1 Peter 5:7: "Cast all your anxiety on him because he cares for you" (NIV).

Another promise of Scripture she claims for her children is from Jeremiah 29: "I know what I'm doing. I have it all planned out–plans to take care of you, not abandon you, plans to give you the future you hope for. When you call on me, when you come and pray to me, I'll listen. When you come looking for me, you'll find me" (vv. 11–13). She also prays Psalm 139, especially verse 13: "For you created my inmost being; you knit me together in my mother's womb" (NIV). She claims this verse for Justus and Noelle, confident that God made them like they are for a reason.

Jason and Nancy also use Psalm 139, but in a different way. Their small son, Sam, is still recovering from brain bleeds that occurred shortly after birth. So they ask God to *continue* to knit Sam together and to give him strength, peace, and comfort for what lies ahead. "We apply John 9:3 to Sam, too," Nancy says. "We pray that the work of God might be displayed in him."

Colleen's daughter Chloe survived two years of cancer treatment as a young teen and wants to move past it. Her mother asks God to use His faithfulness in Chloe's life story to help others who are going through the struggle of cancer. She says, "I also pray that she will know how strong she is in her spirit. She can do anything she sets her mind to."

LeAndre has specific prayer requests for her son Joe, who has autism and cerebral palsy, both complications of his premature birth. "I pray for his perseverance through adversity, that he will be tenacious without being unpleasant." She often begins her prayers with

Three More Ways to Pray for Your Child

- Pray that the fruits of the Spirit listed in Galatians 5:22–23, love, joy, peace, patience, kindness, goodness, faithfulness, gentleness, and self-control, will be evident in your child's life.
- Use "Thirty Ways to Pray for Your Children's Character" in appendix A.
- Use "Thirty Scriptures to Pray for Your Children" in appendix A.

James 5:16: "The prayer of a person living right with God is something powerful to be reckoned with." She prays that Joe will obey Jesus' command from the gospel of Matthew: "Whoever wants to be my disciple must deny themselves and take up their cross and follow me" (Matthew 16:24 NIV).

Kylie's parents began praying Colossians 1:9–12 shortly before they had her evaluated. Since their daughter's diagnosis of autism, they continue to pray these verses:

> So we have continued praying for you ever since we first heard about you. We ask God to give you a complete understanding of what He wants to do in your [life], and we ask him to make you wise with spiritual wisdom. Then the way you live will always honor and please the Lord, and you will continually do good, kind things for others. All the while, you will learn to know God better and better. We also pray that you will be strengthened with his glorious power so that you will have all the patience and endurance you need. May you be filled with joy, always thanking the Father, who has enabled you to share the inheritance that belongs to God's holy people, who live in the light. (New Living Translation, 1996)

What beautiful words to pray over any child! What rich promises they hold for parents of kids with special needs. When we offer up God's promises in faith on behalf of our children, we can trust Him to fulfill them—even when He seems slow to answer.

Selecting Other Resources

Praying for children is essential. So is sharing your faith by talking with them about how God is working in your life. The challenge isn't finding resources to guide you but selecting the ones most appropriate for your child's needs. When looking for materials, remember that you are the expert on your child, and you can best determine

Five Ways to Adapt Materials for Your Kids

1. Alter the Learning Style: Take advantage of the how your child learns best. Sing the lesson, draw, role-play, conduct experiments, or chant.
2. Keep It Moving: Break up the lesson by creating a routine of standing up or sitting down, clapping, or marching in rhythm at natural break points.
3. Make It a Game: Present the lesson in a game format. Adaptations of Pictionary and Who Wants to Be a Millionaire are kid-friendly favorites.
4. Take Turns as Leader: Ask your child to prepare and present the lesson to you.
5. Involve the Senses: Most traditional lessons are geared to hearing and sight. Try employing smell, taste, and touch when you can.
6. Apply It to Real Life: Brainstorm ways the lesson applies to real-life situations and follow through on application together. Afterward, discuss what worked and what didn't.

how to capture and maintain your child's interest. Amazon is a good place to start your search, though browsing at the bookstore gives you an opportunity to test books with your children.

Don't limit your search to resources written specifically for people with special needs. If a book's content is about your child's passion or a devotional presents lessons in a unique way, you might be able to adapt them. Above are some ideas to get you started.

Here are descriptions of a few family-friendly, atypical resources:

- For kids who enjoy meaty discussions, Nancy Guthrie's *One Year of Dinner Table Devotions and Discussion Starters* is a good choice.

- Kids who like to be actively involved in a story may enjoy *The One Year Choose Your Own Ending Devotions.*
- If your family wants a read-through-the-Bible-in-a-year-plan, New Life Journals come in several family-friendly versions. The adult reading plan will take parents through the Bible in a year. Kids and teens read pared down portions of each day's text, adjusted for their ages. The journals also provide space for written reflection on the day's reading.
- Teens and adults with developmental delays may relate to the Bible studies and other resources created by Friendship Ministries.

Resting in the Truth

Whatever resources and strategies you choose, you can rest in God's truth about our children. They are a gift from God. Our job is to love them, care for them, and share our faith. His job is to complete the work He began when He knit them together in their mothers' wombs. We can trust God to continue His good work by drawing our children closer to Him throughout their lives. We can trust Him to guide our parenting efforts and hear our prayers.

Best of all, we can look forward to the completion of His magnificent promises. We can look forward to spending eternity with our children, all dressed up in their new bodies, whole and complete. We can look forward to praising the God who, through our children and their special needs, showed us the depths of Christ's compassion and the abundance of His grace.

Until that great day, we can echo the words of Paul in 2 Corinthians 9:15: "Thank God for this gift, his gift. No language can praise it enough!"

"Thanks be to God," we can joyfully say as God unfolds His dreams for our children. "Thanks be to God for the gift of my child. I don't have words to praise you enough!"

Dear God of grace, you have given us this child to raise and teach. Help me live my faith in ways that will draw my child to you. Open my child's eyes to see you and her heart to love you. I trust you, who gave my child life and breath, to grant saving faith and eternal life.

How can I live my faith before my child? How can I make my faith real to my child? What resources can help me? What Scriptures will I pray on behalf of my child?

Take Time to Reflect

Resources

Books

- Paul Miller, *The Praying Life* (NavPress, 2009).
- Nancy Guthrie, *One Year of Dinner Table Devotions and Discussion Starters: 365 Opportunities to Grow Closer to God as a Family* (Tyndale, 2008).
- *The One Year Choose Your Own Ending Devotions* (Tyndale, 2010).

Curriculum and Materials

- New Life Journals for adults, adolescents, and kids: www.life journal.cc
- Friendship Ministries: www.friendship.org
- For information about the curriculum that is an outgrowth of Kim's Sunday school class, go to www.seejesus.net.

- For more techniques and strategies for adapting materials to your child's needs, visit Katie Wetherbee's website *Diving for Pearls* at www.katiewetherbee.wordpress.com.

Conclusion

The parents who told their stories in *Different Dream Parenting* care deeply for you though they haven't met you. They eagerly related their experiences because they know how challenging and rewarding it is to raise a child with special needs. They shared the wisdom and faith they gained during their journeys as caregivers because they don't want you to travel solo. They know you need a great big family to cheer you on.

They also want you to know they are doing more than cheering for you along the way. They're making this journey with you, because that's what family members do. You can stay in touch with many of them at www.DifferentDream.com. Some of them guest blog regularly at the website. Others leave occasional comments about the posts, product reviews, devotions, and resources featured there. Plus, you can interact with other parents and professionals in the special needs community, too.

So stop by for a visit. Post comments, share your expertise, and leave suggestions about future topics you want to see covered. Hearing from you will be a blessing to those who contributed to *Different Dream Parenting* and to me.

On behalf of all of us, welcome to the family!

Appendix A

Prayer Guides

Thirty Prayers of Dependence

Day 1 If God hadn't been there for me, I never would have made it. The minute I said, "I'm slipping, I'm falling," your love, God, took hold and held me fast. (Psalm 94:17–18)
Lord God, this diagnosis makes me feel like I'm falling. Hold me and my child fast in your love.

Day 2 I am God, the only God you've had or ever will have—incomparable, irreplaceable—from the very beginning telling you what the ending will be, all along letting you in on what is going to happen, assuring you, "I'm in this for the long haul, I'll do exactly what I set out to do." (Isaiah 46:9–10)
Father God, I trust your promise to be with us for the long haul because in the beginning you promised to send your Son to save us, and you did. I'll depend on you.

Day 3 For whatever was written in earlier times was written for our instruction, so that through perseverance and the encouragement of the Scriptures we might have hope. (Romans 15:4 NASB)

God in heaven, it's hard to believe a book written thousands of years ago is relevant today, but I need encouragement to persevere for my child. Use your Word to teach me perseverance.

Day 4 God told me, "Don't say, 'I'm only a boy.' I'll tell you where to go and you'll go there. I'll tell you what to say and you'll say it. Don't be afraid of a soul. I'll be right there, looking after you." (Jeremiah 1:7–8)

God, I'm only a young parent. I can't do this unless you tell me what to say, unless you are with me. Give me faith to trust your promise to be with me always.

Day 5 I would have despaired unless I had believed that I would see the goodness of the Lord in the land of the living. Wait for the Lord; be strong and let your heart take courage; yes, wait for the Lord. (Psalm 27:13–14 NASB)

Dear God, I am in despair about my child's diagnosis. Give me strength to believe in your goodness. Give me courage to wait for you to act.

Day 6 God is keeping careful watch over us and the future. The Day is coming when you'll have it all–life healed and whole. I know how great this makes you feel, even though you have to put up with every kind of aggravation in the meantime. (1 Peter 1:5–6)

Father in heaven, is what you're saying true? Will there be a Day when wholeness and health returns to my child? Help me hang on to this promise in hard times.

Day 7 Whenever we're sick and in bed, God becomes our nurse, nurses us back to health. (Psalm 41:3)
Lord, my heart is sick about my child's condition. Nurse me back to health so I can face the future well and strong.

Day 8 I know what I'm doing. I have it all planned out–plans to take care of you, not abandon you, plans to give you the future you hope for. When you call on me, when you come and pray to me, I'll listen. When you come looking for me, you'll find me. (Jeremiah 29:11–13)
God, it's hard to trust your plans for my child, to believe you haven't abandoned us. I'm praying to you. I'm looking for you. When will I find you?

Day 9 The Lord is my light and my salvation; whom shall I fear? The Lord is the defense of my life; whom shall I dread? (Psalm 27:1 NASB)
Father of light, without you I am defenseless and fearful. Be with me today. Be my light. Remind me of your great salvation. Take away my dread.

Day 10 I can do all things through Him who strengthens me. (Philippians 4:13 NASB)
Lord God, I feel like I can't do anything to change my child's situation. Show me all the things I can do today and give me strength to do them.

Day 11 Pray all the time; thank God no matter what happens. This is the way God wants you who belong to Christ Jesus to live. (1 Thessalonians 5:17–18)
Father God, thank you for showing me what I can do for my child. Remind me to pray when I'm stressed. Open my eyes to see your gifts.

Day 12   We continue to shout our praise even when we're hemmed in with troubles, because we know how troubles can develop passionate patience in us, and how that patience in turn forges the tempered steel of virtue, keeping us alert for whatever God will do next. (Romans 5:3–4)

Lord, you don't ask me to praise you for this trouble but to praise you for how you will use it. So I praise you for teaching me patience, virtue, and whatever lesson comes next.

Day 13   All praise to the God and Father of our Master, Jesus the Messiah! Father of all mercy! God of all healing counsel! He comes alongside us when we go through hard times, and before you know it, he brings us alongside someone else who is going through hard times so that we can be there for that person just as God was there for us. (2 Corinthians 1:3–4)

God, come alongside me today. Make me sure of your presence so I can share your hope with someone who needs to hear about it.

Day 14   The spacious, free life is from God, it's also protected and safe. God-strengthened, we're delivered from evil—when we run to him, he saves us. (Psalm 37:39–40)

Lord, my child is weak and defenseless. I can't picture him having the life of freedom you promise. Give me strength to pick up my child and run to you when I am attacked by despair.

Day 15   So then it does not depend on the man who wills or the man who runs, but on God who has mercy. (Romans 9:16 NASB)

Jesus, what a relief to know that my child's life depends on your great mercy, not my frail intellect and actions. Have mercy on us today!

Day 16 Don't quit in hard times; pray all the harder. (Romans 12:12)

God, life is so hard for my child and for me. I want to give up. I want to quit, but then who would be my child's voice? Give me a heart to pray all the harder.

Day 17 God's my island hideaway, keeps danger far from the shore, throws garlands of hosannas around my neck. (Psalm 32:7)

Rock of Ages, I would love to get away and relax for a few days. A tropical island would be nice, but you are better. Be my hiding place today and restore my heart.

Day 18 Keep your eyes on Jesus, who both began and finished this race we're in. Study how he did it. . . . When you find yourselves flagging in your faith, go over that story again, item by item, that long litany of hostility he plowed through. That will shoot adrenaline into your souls! (Hebrews 12:2–3)

Jesus, when I take my eyes off you, my energy and stamina drain away. Stand before me so I can meditate on what you have done. Be the energy I need.

Day 19 If your revelation hadn't delighted me so, I would have given up when the hard times came. But I'll never forget the advice you gave me; you saved my life with those wise words. (Psalm 119:92–93)

Dear God, hearing the doctor diagnose our child's condition was so hard. But your Word has strengthened my heart and saved my life in the past, so I won't give up.

Day 20 He knows us far better than we know ourselves, knows our pregnant condition, and keeps us present before

God. That's why we can be so sure that every detail in our lives of love for God is worked into something good. (Romans 8:27–28)

Dear Father, human knowledge is so limited. I would be hopeless if I didn't believe a God exists who can work good in this hard situation. Help me trust you to do good.

Day 21 Examine me, God, from head to foot, order your battery of tests. Make sure I'm fit inside and out so I never lose sight of your love, but keep in step with you, never missing a beat. (Psalm 26:2–3)

Great Physician, examine my battered and wounded heart. Heal me so I'm fit to follow you through this journey with my child.

Day 22 Now I take limitations in stride, and with good cheer, these limitations that cut me down to size—abuse, accidents, opposition, bad breaks. I just let Christ take over! And so the weaker I get, the stronger I become. (2 Corinthians 12:10)

God, if you sent this situation to reveal my weakness, you'll have to take over and show me how to keep moving ahead. I can't do it myself.

Day 23 Is there anyone around who can explain God? Anyone smart enough to tell him what to do? Anyone who has done him such a huge favor that God has to ask his advice? Everything comes from him; everything happens through him; everything ends up in him. Always glory! Always praise! Yes. Yes. Yes. (Romans 11:34–36)

Dear Lord of the universe, you are vast and I am small. You know all things, and I know so little. Forgive me for telling you what to do. May I trust you to accomplish all things.

Day 24   I'm sure now I'll see God's goodness in the exuberant earth. Stay with God! Take heart. Don't quit. I'll say it again: Stay with God. (Psalm 27:13–14)

Creator God, it's hard to believe in you when my child is suffering. Show me your goodness so I won't give up on you.

Day 25   Friends, when life gets really difficult, don't jump to the conclusion that God isn't on the job. Instead, be glad that you are in the very thick of what Christ experienced. This is a spiritual refining process, with glory just around the corner. (1 Peter 4:12–13)

God of glory, after I received my child's diagnosis, I was sure you'd abandoned us. Keep my mind on your Son's past sufferings and future glory so I can trust you today.

Day 26   Cease striving and know that I am God. (Psalm 46:10 NASB)

Father, I want to make my child better. I want to yell at someone. I want to argue with you. Settle my spirit so I can rest and know you are really God.

Day 27   Dear God, my Master, you created earth and sky by your great power—by merely stretching out your arm! There is nothing you can't do. (Jeremiah 32:17)

Creator of all things, you can do anything. I can do nothing. Change my child's condition, or work through it to accomplish great good.

Day 28   Every good thing given and every perfect gift is from above, coming down from the Father of lights, with whom there is no variation or shifting shadow. (James 1:17 NASB)

Dear Father of lights, give me eyes to see the good and perfect work you are doing in my child's life.

Day 29 I'll say no more, I'll shut my mouth, since you, Lord, are behind all this. But I can't take it much longer. (Psalm 39:9–10)

God, if I open my mouth, I fear what will come out. If you are there, if you are truly in control of this situation, send help. I'm too exhausted and broken to go on alone.

Day 30 Let's keep a firm grip on the promises that keep us going. He always keeps his word. (Hebrews 10:23)

God, I am so weak, I can barely cling to your promises. Use the promise that you keep your word to give my family hope today.

Thirty Prayers for a Hospital Stay

Day 1 Be assured that from the first day we heard of you, we haven't stopped praying for you, asking God to give you wise minds and spirits attuned to his will, and so acquire a thorough understanding of the ways in which God works. (Colossians 1:9)

Dear Father, thank you for the people caring for my child in this hospital. Give them wise minds and spirits to follow your will. Use my interactions to show workers how Christ is at work in me.

Day 2 But I'll take the hand of those who don't know the way, who can't see where they're going. I'll be a personal guide to them, directing them through unknown country. I'll be right there to show them what roads to take, make sure they don't fall into the ditch. These are the things I'll be doing for them—sticking with them, not leaving them for a minute. (Isaiah 42:16)

Lord, many people working with my child don't know you or your ways. But you are bigger than their lack of vision. So guide their medical decisions. Be with them and with my child every minute of the day.

Day 3 The fundamental fact of existence is that this trust in God, this faith, is the firm foundation under everything that makes life worth living. It's our handle on what we can't see. (Hebrews 11:1)

Father in heaven, open our eyes to what we can't see. Open the eyes of my child's doctors and nurses so trust in you becomes their foundation too.

Day 4 You will make known to me the path of life; in Your presence is fullness of joy; in Your right hand there are pleasures forever. (Psalm 16:11 NASB)

Jesus, you are the path of life. Become the path of life for the dear people caring for my child. May they find pleasure in your presence.

Day 5 God is good, a hiding place in tough times. He recognizes and welcomes anyone looking for help. (Nahum 1:7)

Good Father, be my hiding place during this tough time. When the workers in this hospital are stressed and in need of help, welcome them into your hiding place too.

Day 6 I know, God, that mere mortals can't run their own lives, that men and women don't have what it takes to take charge of life. So correct us, God, as you see best. Don't lose your temper. That would be the end of us. (Jeremiah 10:23–24)

Sovereign God, I believe in you, but it's still hard for me to admit I'm not in control of my life. Have mercy on me. Have mercy on the people in this place who don't know you, who think they are in charge of their lives. Gently correct them. Show them who you are.

Day 7

People with their minds set on you, you keep completely whole, steady on their feet, because they keep at it and don't quit. (Isaiah 26:3)

Father God, set my mind completely on you so my spirit can be whole and strong. Steady the feet of my child's caregivers. Give each worker strength to persevere until your will for my child is accomplished.

Day 8

"Not by might nor by power, but by My Spirit," says the Lord of hosts. (Zechariah 4:6 NASB)

Lord God, only your Spirit heals body and soul. By your Spirit, guide the minds and hands of the doctors and nurses. By your Spirit, make my child whole in your eyes.

Day 9

You can be sure that God will take care of everything you need, his generosity exceeding even yours in the glory that pours from Jesus. (Philippians 4:19)

God who provides, this hospital stay is revealing my emptiness. How can I care for my child when I have nothing to give? All I can do is trust you to meet my needs in ways that reveal your amazing power.

Day 10

Keep your eyes open for God, watch for his works; be alert for signs of his presence. (Psalm 105:4)

Sustaining God, make me sensitive to your Spirit. Open my eyes to your presence so I will recognize you and find hope. Give me words to tell my child how you are watching over us today.

Day 11   Be strong. Take courage. Don't be intimidated. Don't give them a second thought because God, your God, is striding ahead of you. He's right there with you. He won't let you down; he won't leave you. (Deuteronomy 31:6)

Father of all, I don't understand half of what the doctors and nurses are saying. They know so much more than I do. Be with me. Walk the halls with me. Give me courage to ask questions and make suggestions.

Day 12   And everyone gathered here will learn that God doesn't save by means of sword or spear. The battle belongs to God. (1 Samuel 17:47)

Lord God, the doctors use scalpels and the nurses bring needles, but you are the power over and in them. Remind me often that the battle for my child's health belongs to you alone.

Day 13   By yourself you're unprotected. With a friend you can face the worst. Can you round up a third? A three-stranded rope isn't easily snapped. (Ecclesiastes 4:12)

God of fellowship, the hospital is making me crazy. I am so lonely. Stir my friends to call or visit. Give me the courage to reach out to other parents here.

Day 14   Blessed is he who has regard for the weak; the Lord delivers him in times of trouble. . . . The Lord will sustain him on his sickbed and restore him from his bed of illness. (Psalm 41:1–3 NIV)

Father God, the hospital is a scary place for a child who is sick and in pain. Hold my little one close. Breathe hope and peace into both of us during this hospital visit.

Day 15 How blessed is the man who finds wisdom and the man who gains understanding. (Proverbs 3:13 NASB)
God of all wisdom, bless the doctors and nurses with wisdom and understanding as they care for my child. May they recognize you as the source of their wisdom.

Day 16 Let us choose for ourselves what is right; let us know among ourselves what is good. (Job 34:4 NASB)
Dear Father, no person can choose rightly or recognize good without your guidance. Guide the doctors to choose what you have determined is right for my child.

Day 17 All of you, clothe yourselves with humility toward one another, for God is opposed to the proud, but gives grace to the humble. (1 Peter 5:5 NASB)
Lord of power, grant me a humble heart to trust you as much as my child trusts me. Clothe the powerful people in this hospital with humility so you can work through them and not against them.

Day 18 Give instruction to a wise man and he will be still wiser, teach a righteous man and he will increase his learning. (Proverbs 9:9 NASB)
Righteous God, reveal to me the people who should be on my child's care team. May I recognize those who will listen to my observations and use them to improve treatment.

Day 19 So this is my prayer: that your love will flourish and that you will not only love much but well. Learn to love appropriately. You need to use your head and test your feelings so that your love is sincere and intelligent, not sentimental gush. (Philippians 1:9–10)

Lord, grant a flourishing, intelligent love to all those working with my child. May we all use our heads and not be carried away by feelings.

Day 20 Treat one another justly. Love your neighbors. Be compassionate with each other. (Zechariah 7:9)

God of love, give me your strength to be kind to everyone I meet here. Show me how to love the other parents. Keep me from being so wrapped up in my child's struggles that I forget to show compassion to others.

Day 21 God is a safe place to hide, ready to help when we need him. (Psalm 46:1)

Lord, with my child in the hospital, it's hard for me to trust you to keep us safe. But you promise to be a hiding place and a help. Be both for my family today.

Day 22 So speak encouraging words to one another. Build up hope so you'll all be together in this, no one left out, no one left behind. I know you're already doing this; just keep on doing it. (1 Thessalonians 5:11)

Jesus, Word of God, I want to be an encourager for my child and for the health care workers. Put your words into my mouth, words of hope and encouragement, to keep us going when the days are difficult.

Day 23 They came together in a coalition to fight against Joshua and Israel under a single command. (Joshua 9:2)

God who reigns over all, make the members of the care team into a single-minded unit that fights together to do what is best in your eyes for my child.

Day 24 Into the hovels of the poor, into the dark streets where the homeless groan, God speaks: "I've had enough; I'm

on my way to heal the ache in the heart of the wretched."
(Psalm 12:5)

Compassionate Father, thank you for being present with us in heartache and wretchedness. Hear the groanings of the families crying out to you in this place. Heal our spirits and the spirits of our children.

Day 25 Kind words heal and help; cutting words wound and maim. (Proverbs 15:4)

Merciful God, before I speak, remind me of the power of words. Even when I have reason to be angry, calm my spirit so my words convey healing and help.

Day 26 Do you see it now? Do you see that I'm the one? Do you see that there's no other god beside me? I bring death and I give life, I wound and I heal—there is no getting away from or around me! (Deuteronomy 32:39)

Oh God, thank you for your reminder of who controls my child's life. Thank you for bearing this burden I'm too weak to handle. Give me faith to rest in your plans for my precious child.

Day 27 But now take another look. I'm going to give this city a thorough renovation, working a true healing inside and out. I'm going to show them life whole, life brimming with blessings. (Jeremiah 33:6)

Lord God, so many people in this hospital don't know you. Draw them to yourself. Renovate their hearts. Grant them spiritual healing, and the blessed hope of eternal life in you.

Day 28 I'll give you a new heart. I'll put a new spirit in you. I'll cut out your stone heart and replace it with a red-blooded, firm-muscled heart. Then you'll obey my statutes and be careful to obey my commands. You'll be my people! I'll be your God! (Ezekiel 11:19–20)

Lord God, thank you for the people here who love and care for my child. They have become dear to us. Touch the hearts of those who don't know you and give them hearts eager to follow after and obey you.

Day 29 Are there no healing ointments in Gilead? Isn't there a doctor in the house? So why can't something be done to heal and save my dear, dear people? (Jeremiah 8:22)

Healing God, this hospital is full of doctors who heal the sick and bind up wounds. But only you offer healing balm to save souls for eternity. Pour out your healing on hospital workers, patients, and families who don't yet know you.

Day 30 God has rolled up his sleeves. All the nations can see his holy, muscled arm. Everyone, from one end of the earth to the other, sees him at work, doing his salvation work. (Isaiah 52:10)

Father God, I see you rolling up your sleeves and doing your healing work in this hospital. May the patients, their families, and all the people employed here see you not only restoring bodies, but also doing your eternal work of salvation.

Thirty Ways to Pray for Your Family

Day 1 What marvelous love the Father has extended to us! Just look at it—we're called children of God! . . . And that's only the beginning. Who knows how we'll end up! What we know is that when Christ is openly revealed, we'll see him—and in seeing him, become like him. (1 John 3:1–2)

Dear God, thank you for being my Father and for not being finished with me yet. Help my family reflect your relationship with your Son until the day He comes again, and we see Him as He is.

Day 2 Like a shepherd, he will care for his flock, gathering the lambs in his arms, hugging them as he carries them, leading the nursing ewes to good pasture. (Isaiah 40:11)
Good Shepherd, have mercy on my family, your lambs. Hold my children close in your arms while you lead me to good pastures filled with what we need.

Day 3 Yes, I've settled on him as the one to train his children and future family to observe God's way of life, live kindly and generously and fairly, so that God can complete in Abraham what he promised him. (Genesis 18:19)
God who chose Abraham, I don't know why you chose me to parent my children, to train them to observe your ways. But because you promise to complete whatever you begin, I have your confidence to teach them how to live kind, generous, and righteous lives.

Day 4 If we go through the hard times with him, then we're certainly going to go through the good times with him! That's why I don't think there's any comparison between the present hard times and the coming good times. (Romans 8:17–18)
Jesus, you went through hard times while you were on earth, and you promised better times ahead. That's why my family is moving forward despite the challenges of special needs. We believe your promise and look forward to what's to come.

Day 5 Don't be obsessed with getting more material things. Be relaxed with what you have. Since God assured us, "I'll never let you down, never walk off and leave you," we can boldly quote, God is there, ready to help; I'm fearless no matter what. Who or what can get to me? (Hebrews 13:5–6)

Dear Provider, when time is short and money is tight, it's hard to believe you are with us. But you are there. You are protecting us. Please, Lord, meet our needs.

Day 6   But we're not quitters who lose out. Oh, no! We'll stay with it and survive, trusting all the way. (Hebrews 10:39)

Lord God, some days I am tempted to give up. But what kind of example would that be for my children? Give me faith to persevere so my kids will see how to survive by faith.

Day 7   By your words I can see where I'm going; they throw a beam of light on my dark path. (Psalm 119:105)

Word of God, in the Bible you say that your Word is a believer's guiding light. Give me motivation to gather my family to read and study it together often.

Day 8   That clinches it—help's coming, an answer's on the way, everything's going to work out. See those people polishing their chariots, and those others grooming their horses? But we're making garlands for God our God. The chariots will rust, those horses pull up lame—and we'll be on our feet, standing tall. (Psalm 20:6–8)

Strong Deliverer, sometimes the onslaught of daily demands feels like an attack. But you promise to help. Please send help to keep me standing when I feel overwhelmed by the needs of my family.

Day 9   Look at me and help me! I'm all alone and in big trouble. My heart and kidneys are fighting each other; call a truce to this civil war. (Psalm 25:16–17)

Lord, I need your help. I'm being pulled in so many directions. I want to do everything and please everyone. But I can't, so show me your will for my family this day so the war within me will cease.

Day 10 That goes for all of you, no exceptions. No retaliation. No sharp-tongued sarcasm. Instead, bless—that's your job, to bless. You'll be a blessing and also get a blessing. (1 Peter 3:9)
Giver of Breath, the life you breathe into us is a blessing. My child is a blessing. Show me how to bless my child and to recognize each blessing you settle on my family.

Day 11 The suffering won't last forever. It won't be long before this generous God who has great plans for us in Christ—eternal and glorious plans they are!—will have you put together and on your feet for good. (1 Peter 5:10)
Eternal God, some days it is so hard to look beyond our present challenges to your hope. Sustain us until that day comes. Calm our hearts. Put us on our feet.

Day 12 God's a safe-house for the battered, a sanctuary during bad times. The moment you arrive, you relax; you're never sorry you knocked. (Psalm 9:9–10)
God of sanctuary, I don't know when or if these special needs obstacles will end, but your Word says you are a safe house for battered people. Walk my family through your doors so we can relax in your arms.

Day 13 Consider it a sheer gift, friends, when tests and challenges come at you from all sides. You know that under pressure, your faith-life is forced into the open and shows its true colors. So don't try to get out of anything prematurely. Let it do its work so you become mature and well-developed, not deficient in any way. (James 1:2–4)

God, you are determined to mature our family, aren't you? The pressures of raising a child with special needs force us to live our faith and grow. But we can only continue doing this if you hold us close during the painful maturing process.

Day 14 Make this your common practice: Confess your sins to each other and pray for each other so that you can live together whole and healed. The prayer of a person living right with God is something powerful to be reckoned with. (James 5:16)

Forgiving God, give everyone in my family courage to confess sins so we can forgive one another and be whole. Give us compassion to pray for one another every day.

Day 15 God is a safe place to hide, ready to help when we need him. (Psalm 46:1)

Dear God, some days I am so tired and scared I want to hide from the demands of parenting. Show me how to hide in your promised safe place and be present with my family at the same time.

Day 16 As parents feel for their children, God feels for those who fear him. He knows us inside and out, keeps in mind that we're made of mud. (Psalm 103:13–14)

Dear Father, it's hard to believe you could love me as much as I love my kids when you know my bitter thoughts, my doubts, my anger. I bow in the presence of your compassion and grace. May I show your grace to my family.

Day 17   Give your entire attention to what God is doing right now, and don't get worked up about what may or may not happen tomorrow. God will help you deal with whatever hard things come up when the time comes. (Matthew 6:34)

Dear God of the present, when I think about my child's special needs and the future, I am overwhelmed. Teach me to be present with my family today and to trust that you will help me deal with what lies ahead.

Day 18   These hard times are small potatoes compared to the coming good times, the lavish celebration prepared for us. There's far more here than meets the eye. The things we see now are here today, gone tomorrow. But the things we can't see now will last forever. (2 Corinthians 4:17–18)

Lord of all eternity, the challenges facing my child seem huge right now. Give us both eyes to see beyond this life. Give us feet to stand on your eternal promises. Give us hope.

Day 19   Don't fret or worry. Instead of worrying, pray. Let petitions and praises shape your worries into prayers, letting God know your concerns. (Philippians 4:6)

Dear God who answers prayer, will you wave a red flag when I begin to worry? Stop me in my tracks, so I can turn my worries into prayers. Nudge me to share all my concerns with you.

Day 20   "I don't think the way you think. The way you work isn't the way I work." God's Decree. "For as the sky soars high above earth, so the way I work surpasses the way you work, and the way I think is beyond the way you think." (Isaiah 55:8–9)

God of wisdom, I am so thankful that even when I don't understand what's happening to my child and our family, you do. Give me faith in your plan, which is far superior to anything I could devise.

Day 21 Don't panic. I'm with you. There's no need to fear for I'm your God. I'll give you strength. I'll help you. I'll hold you steady, keep a firm grip on you. (Isaiah 41:10)
Dear Lord, you tell me not to panic, but it is so hard to stay calm when I think of my family's needs. Wrap your arms around us, steady us, hold us. Keep me from being fearful so my children won't be afraid.

Day 22 Don't bargain with God. Be direct. Ask for what you need. (Matthew 7:7)
Dear Provider, you say not to bargain with you but to ask for what my family needs. I need you to show me how to handle this child or bring someone to help us.

Day 23 God's name is a place of protection—good people can run there and be safe. (Proverbs 18:10)
God of protection, if you are the safe place you say you are, I want to run to you and be safe. Give my family time to spend in your Word, so my child will run to you and be safe too.

Day 24 Whatever I have, wherever I am, I can make it through anything in the One who makes me who I am. (Philippians 4:13)
Dear Creator, you made everyone in my family who we are: wives, husbands, sons, daughters. So I claim your promise to lead us through whatever lies ahead, wherever we are.

Day 25 When I get really afraid I come to you in trust. I'm proud to praise God; fearless now, I trust in God. What can mere mortals do? (Psalm 56:3–4)
Dear Lord, train every person in my family to come to you when we are afraid. Show us how much stronger you are than humans, so we become fearless and praise you always.

Day 26 God, the one and only—I'll wait as long as he says. Everything I hope for comes from him, so why not? He's solid rock under my feet, breathing room for my soul, an impregnable castle: I'm set for life. (Psalm 62:5–6)
Dear God, you are using my child with special needs to teach me patience, aren't you? I will wait, confident that in you we can meet every challenge of life. Please teach my child patience too.

Day 27 If God doesn't build the house, the builders only build shacks. If God doesn't guard the city, the night watchman might as well nap. (Psalm 127:1)
Dear Builder of our house, your Word says my family must be built on you, or it won't stand. Work in our hearts so we all claim you as Lord of this house.

Day 28 Friends love through all kinds of weather, and families stick together in all kinds of trouble. (Proverbs 17:17)
Dear God of our family, you created families to stick together. Be the glue that holds us together in good times and bad so our children will trust you as their Lord and Savior.

Day 29 Let the peace of Christ keep you in tune with each other, in step with each other. None of this going off and doing your own thing. And cultivate thankfulness. Let the Word of Christ—the Message—have the run of the house. Give it plenty of room in your lives. Instruct and direct one another using good common sense. And sing, sing your hearts out to God! (Colossians 3:15–16)

Dear Christ, fill this house with your peace, your song. Bind us together as a family, thankful and supportive, obedient to your Word. Show me how to live my faith so my children learn to trust you.

Day 30 Listen to me, family of Jacob, everyone that's left of the family of Israel. I've been carrying you on my back from the day you were born, and I'll keep on carrying you when you're old. I'll be there, bearing you when you're old and gray. I've done it and will keep on doing it, carrying you on my back, saving you. (Isaiah 46:3–4)

Mighty God, I am too tired to meet my family's needs tonight. Would you carry me, as you have carried me since birth? Will you carry my family too, and save us during this adjustment to life with special needs?

Thirty Prayers for Educators and Therapists

Day 1 In all their troubles, he was troubled, too. He didn't send someone else to help them. He did it himself, in person. Out of his own love and pity he redeemed them. He rescued them and carried them along for a long, long time. (Isaiah 63:9)

Dear Father, when my child's teachers are troubled, please rescue them. Make yourself known to them as the one who carries them through difficult times.

Day 2 Trust God from the bottom of your heart; don't try to figure out everything on your own. Listen for God's voice in everything you do, everywhere you go; he's the one who will keep you on track. Don't assume that you know it all. Run to God! Run from evil! (Proverbs 3:5–7)

Dear God of wisdom, give teachers ears to hear your voice. Give them hearts dependent on your wisdom. Give them feet to run to you when they need answers.

Day 3

God can do anything, you know—far more than you could ever imagine or guess or request in your wildest dreams! He does it not by pushing us around but by working within us, his Spirit deeply and gently within us. (Ephesians 3:20)

Holy Spirit, you are at work everywhere in my child's school, doing more than I can imagine. I trust you to work deeply and gently within teachers and other school workers.

Day 4

God is always on the alert, constantly on the lookout for people who are totally committed to him. (2 Chronicles 16:9)

Dear God who sees all things, you know which teachers and staff members love you. Surround my child with adults who are committed to you and to kids with special needs.

Day 5

But because God was so gracious, so very generous, here I am. And I'm not about to let his grace go to waste. Haven't I worked hard trying to do more than any of the others? Even then, my work didn't amount to all that much. It was God giving me the work to do, God giving me the energy to do it. (1 Corinthians 15:10)

God of grace, open the eyes of teachers and educators to your grace so they won't let it go to waste. May their hearts be grateful for meaningful work. Give them energy each day to work with the children in their classrooms.

Day 6   God is striding ahead of you. He's right there with you. He won't let you down; he won't leave you. Don't be intimidated. Don't worry. (Deuteronomy 31:8)
Dear God with us, show my child's teachers that you are with them. Be their confidence when their jobs are hard. Be their boldness when they advocate for students.

Day 7   The person who trusts me will not only do what I'm doing but even greater things, because I, on my way to the Father, am giving you the same work to do that I've been doing. You can count on it. (John 14:12)
Dear Jesus, I trust you to do great things at my child's school through me and my child. Show us the work you have for us to complete in the lives of the students, teachers, and staff.

Day 8   God gives out Wisdom free, is plainspoken in Knowledge and Understanding. He's a rich mine of Common Sense for those who live well, a personal bodyguard to the candid and sincere. (Proverbs 2:6–7)
God of wisdom, be a rich mine of common sense for the workers in my child's school. Grant them your wisdom, knowledge, and understanding in all their decisions.

Day 9   The revelation of God is whole and pulls our lives together. The signposts of God are clear and point out the right road. (Psalm 19:7)
Dear God of revelation, help my child's teachers recognize your signposts so they will choose your road. Grant them wholeness and full lives in you.

Day 10   I am writing to you, fathers, because you know Him who has been from the beginning. I am writing to you, young men, because you have overcome the evil one.

297

I have written to you, children, because you know the Father. (1 John 2:13 NASB)

Dear Lord and Savior, bring those working in the school to a saving knowledge of you so they will desire to do your will for my child.

Day 11   And then he told me, My grace is enough; it's all you need. My strength comes into its own in your weakness. Once I heard that, I was glad to let it happen. I quit focusing on the handicap and began appreciating the gift. It was a case of Christ's strength moving in on my weakness. (2 Corinthians 12:9)

Dear God who is my strength, may your power give those working with my child strength in their weakness.

Day 12   Your love has given me great joy and encouragement, because you, brother, have refreshed the hearts of the saints. (Philemon 7 NIV)

Dear God who encourages, use me to refresh and encourage teachers and staff members by sharing with them the joy you give me.

Day 13   Make the most of every chance you get. These are desperate times! (Ephesians 5:16)

Dear Lord of time, guide teachers to use the time they have with my child wisely and well.

Day 14   My dear children, let's not just talk about love; let's practice real love. (1 John 3:18)

Dear God of love, may those working with my child love him, not only in word or talk, but in practice.

Day 15   Tune your ears to the world of Wisdom; set your heart on a life of Understanding. (Proverbs 2:2)

Dear God who understands my child's needs, pour your wisdom into the hearts of my child's teachers so they understand her.

Day 16 God created human beings; he created them godlike, reflecting God's nature. (Genesis 1:27)
Dear Creator, may your example of creativity stir creativity in the hearts of those who teach my child.

Day 17 Real wisdom, God's wisdom, begins with a holy life and is characterized by getting along with others. It is gentle and reasonable, overflowing with mercy and blessings, not hot one day and cold the next, not two-faced. (James 3:17)
Dear God of stability, fill teachers with your unchanging wisdom and stability day after day so my child has a consistent environment.

Day 18 God wants us to grow up, to know the whole truth and tell it in love—like Christ in everything. We take our lead from Christ, who is the source of everything we do. (Ephesians 4:15)
Word of God, put truth into the mouths of the teachers and staff. May they speak truth with the love you demonstrated to us through Christ.

Day 19 You can be sure that God will take care of everything you need, his generosity exceeding even yours in the glory that pours from Jesus. (Philippians 4:19)
Dear Lord of provision, supply everything the school requires to meet the needs of all the students.

Day 20 Save your breath for the wise—they'll be wiser for it; tell good people what you know—they'll profit from it. (Proverbs 9:9)

Dear God who sees the heart, help me discern the wise, good people who work with my child. Help me communicate with them about my child's needs so they can teach him effectively.

Day 21 For sound advice is a beacon, good teaching is a light, moral discipline is a life path. (Proverbs 6:23)
Dear Lord of all, thank you for teachers who listen to sound advice, teach well, and dispense moral discipline. May we be partners along my child's life path.

Day 22 May the Master take you by the hand and lead you along the path of God's love and Christ's endurance. (2 Thessalonians 3:5)
Dear Master, hold hands with my child's teachers. Lead them to your love and grant them your Son's endurance as they do the hard work of teaching.

Day 23 What a gift life is to those who stay the course! You've heard, of course, of Job's staying power, and you know how God brought it all together for him at the end. That's because God cares, cares right down to the last detail. (James 5:11)
Dear Lord, give my child's teachers the gift of perseverance today and every day. Show them how you care for every detail of their lives at school and at home.

Day 24 I'll give you a new heart, put a new spirit in you. I'll remove the stone heart from your body and replace it with a heart that's God-willed, not self-willed. I'll put my Spirit in you and make it possible for you to do what I tell you and live by my commands. (Ezekiel 36:26–27)

Dear Jesus, if my child's teacher doesn't have a heart for you, use us to soften her spirit and bring her to you. Fill her with your Spirit so she can obey your commands.

Day 25   Have you ever come on anything quite like this extravagant generosity of God, this deep, deep wisdom? It's way over our heads. We'll never figure it out. (Romans 11:33)

Dear Giver of all good gifts, lavish your deep wisdom on those who work at my child's school. May they worship you, knowing that your wisdom enables them to do what is beyond their ability.

Day 26   Do you want to be counted wise, to build a reputation for wisdom? Here's what you do: Live well, live wisely, live humbly. It's the way you live, not the way you talk, that counts. (James 3:13)

Dear God of life, help me to live a wise and humble faith that is evident in all my interactions at school. May the way I live be a testimony you can use to draw the lost to Christ.

Day 27   And mark that you do this with humility and discipline—not in fits and starts, but steadily, pouring yourselves out for each other in acts of love. (Ephesians 4:2)

Dear Jesus, grant me a humble and disciplined heart so I can consistently shower love on everyone who works with my child at school.

Day 28   No test or temptation that comes your way is beyond the course of what others have had to face. All you need to remember is that God will never let you down; he'll never let you be pushed past your limit; he'll always be there to help you come through it. (1 Corinthians 10:13)

Dear God of power, when my child's teachers face temptation, remind them of your promise to help them through it. Give them the courage and strength to choose rightly.

Day 29 Staying with it—that's what is required. Stay with it to the end. You won't be sorry; you'll be saved. (Luke 21:19)
Dear Persevering One, give my child's teachers power to persevere through days of unrelenting demands from students, parents, and administrators.

Day 30 But you need to stick it out, staying with God's plan so you'll be there for the promised completion. (Hebrews 10:36)
Holy Spirit, put a spirit of endurance in those who work at my child's school. When they are discouraged and want to quit, grant them perseverance to stick with your plan.

Thirty Prayers for Grieving Families

Day 1 Everything's falling apart on me, God; put me together again with your Word. (Psalm 119:107)
Word of God, my child is dying, and my world is falling apart. I am falling apart. Guide me to the truth in your Word that will put me and my life back together again.

Day 2 Meanwhile, the moment we get tired in the waiting, God's Spirit is right alongside helping us along. If we don't know how or what to pray, it doesn't matter. He does our praying in and for us, making prayer out of our wordless sighs, our aching groans. (Romans 8:26)

Dear Holy Spirit, will this burden of grief ever lift? I am so tired I can't think of the words to pray. Please be in my sighs and groans, praying the words you know I need.

Day 3 Job got to his feet, ripped his robe, shaved his head, then fell to the ground and worshiped: Naked I came from my mother's womb, naked I'll return to the womb of the earth. God gives, God takes. God's name be ever blessed. (Job 1:20–21)

God who gives and takes away, I don't know how Job worshiped you after his children died. I don't know how he could bless you after such a loss. All I can do is follow his example and repeat his words: "God gives, God takes. God's name be ever blessed." Now, God, give me faith to believe them.

Day 4 My life's about over. All my plans are smashed, all my hopes are snuffed out. (Job 17:11)

Dear God of hope, I feel like Job. Hopeless. All my dreams and plans broken. My life in ruins. Carry me through this grief and give me a reason to hope again.

Day 5 Still, I know that God lives—the One who gives me back my life—and eventually he'll take his stand on earth. And I'll see him—even though I get skinned alive!—see God myself, with my very own eyes. Oh, how I long for that day! (Job 19:25–27)

Dear Breath of Life, losing a child is like being skinned alive. The only way to bear the pain is by clinging to you, the God who gives life. I look forward to the day when I will see you and my child. How I long for that day!

Day 6 May the words of my mouth and the meditation of my heart be pleasing in your sight, O Lord, my Rock and my Redeemer. (Psalm 19:14 NIV)
Dear Redeemer, all I can think about is the loss of my child. All I can pray about is my grief. This is all I have to offer you today. Accept it and be pleased with it, my Rock and Redeemer.

Day 7 Don't turn a deaf ear when I call you, God. If all I get from you is deafening silence, I'd be better off in the Black Hole. I'm letting you know what I need, calling out for help and lifting my arms toward your inner sanctum. (Psalm 28:1–2)
Dear God, hear my prayer. Speak to me and comfort me in my all-consuming grief. I need you, Lord. I'm calling out to you. Please, answer me.

Day 8 God, God . . . my God! Why did you dump me miles from nowhere? Doubled up with pain, I call to God all the day long. No answer. Nothing. I keep at it all night, tossing and turning. (Psalm 22:1–2)
Lord God, are you there? Why have you abandoned me in my pain? I call to you continually. I need to hear from you. Answer me, God. Send someone to speak your comfort to my family.

Day 9 Even when the way goes through Death Valley, I'm not afraid when you walk at my side. Your trusty shepherd's crook makes me feel secure. (Psalm 23:4)
Good Shepherd, thank you for carrying my child through the valley of death. What a comfort to know my little lamb felt safe and secure in your arms.

Day 10 When I was desperate, I called out, and God got me out of a tight spot. God's angel sets up a circle of protection around us while we pray. (Psalm 34:6–7)

Dear God, I am desperate, overcome with grief as never before. I can't get out of this hole without you. Send your angel to protect me and lift me out of despair.

Day 11 Is anyone crying for help? God is listening, ready to rescue you. If your heart is broken, you'll find God right there; if you're kicked in the gut, he'll help you catch your breath. (Psalm 34:17–18)

Dear Father, I am crying for help and claiming your promise to rescue me. Stay close beside me. Heal this broken heart. Breathe for me until this deep pain eases.

Day 12 He used his servant body to carry our sins to the Cross so we could be rid of sin, free to live the right way. His wounds became your healing. (1 Peter 2:24)

Dear Jesus, you know the pain of death. You were wounded to heal me. May the thought of your sacrifice begin to heal my grief.

Day 13 Be gracious to me, O Lord, for I am pining away; heal me, O Lord, for my bones are dismayed. And my soul is greatly dismayed; but You, O Lord—how long? (Psalm 6:2–3 NASB)

O Lord, my body and soul are sick with grief. I'm not sure how much more I can bear. How long until I feel some relief, God? How long do I have to wait?

Day 14 God will never walk away from his people, never desert his precious people. (Psalm 94:14)

Dear God, your Word says you don't desert your people. But when my child died, it felt like you deserted me. All I can do is cling to your promise and trust that you are there.

Day 15 Create in me a clean heart, O God, and renew a steadfast spirit within me. Do not cast me away from Your presence and do not take Your Holy Spirit from me. Restore to me the joy of Your salvation and sustain me with a willing spirit. (Psalm 51:10–12 NASB)
Dear God of Restoration, grief for my child makes me feel dead inside. Make me feel alive again. Renew my spirit. Walk me through this darkness until I know joy again.

Day 16 Pile your troubles on God's shoulders—he'll carry your load, he'll help you out. He'll never let good people topple into ruin. (Psalm 55:22)
God of strength, I can't carry this loss alone. You promise to carry my load when I can't. Can you bear it for me today? Will you keep me from falling apart completely?

Day 17 I'm on a diet of tears—tears for breakfast, tears for supper. All day long people knock at my door, pestering, "Where is this God of yours?" (Psalm 42:3)
Dear Father, I can't stop crying. People see me crying and ask how a loving God could allow a child to die. How can I answer them? Tell me what to say.

Day 18 You're all I want in heaven! You're all I want on earth! (Psalm 73:25)
Dear Lord, I wish I could say you are all I want. But all I want today is for my child to be alive again. Change my heart so I can once again say you are all I want.

Day 19 I've kept my feet on the ground, I've cultivated a quiet heart. Like a baby content in its mother's arms, my soul is a baby content. Wait, Israel, for God. Wait with hope. Hope now; hope always! (Psalm 131:2–3)

Lord God, I hurt so much today. Hold me close and quiet my heart. Settle my spirit. Ease this grief and be my hope, now and always.

Day 20 The king was stunned. Heartbroken, he went up to the room over the gate and wept. As he wept he cried out, O my son Absalom, my dear, dear son Absalom! Why not me rather than you, my death and not yours, O Absalom, my dear, dear son! (2 Samuel 18:33)

Dear God, why didn't you let me die instead of my child? Why couldn't I bear the pain for her? I am heartbroken by this grief, stunned by the loss. All I can do is cry.

Day 21 God's loyal love couldn't have run out, his merciful love couldn't have dried up. They're created new every morning. How great your faithfulness! I'm sticking with God (I say it over and over). He's all I've got left. (Lamentations 3:22–24)

Lord God, my child is dead. You are all I have left. Keep me close to you. Open my eyes to your mercy and love while I grieve. Show me your faithfulness day after day.

Day 22 If he works severely, he also works tenderly. His stockpiles of loyal love are immense. (Lamentations 3:32)

Dear God of love, you have worked severely in my life by taking away my child. Now I need to know your tenderness and love. Show your love to me today.

Day 23 But now, God's Message, the God who made you in the first place, Jacob, the One who got you started, Israel: "Don't be afraid, I've redeemed you. I've called your name. You're mine. When you're in over your head, I'll be there with you. When you're in rough waters, you will not go down. When you're between a rock and a hard place, it won't be a dead end—because I am God, your personal God, The Holy of Israel, your Savior." (Isaiah 43:1–3)

Dear God of Israel, I need a huge God to rescue me from this raging river of grief. I need you to save me today like you saved Israel. Lift me up. Keep me from drowning.

Day 24 This is for keeps, a life-or-death fight to the finish against the Devil and all his angels. Be prepared. You're up against far more than you can handle on your own. Take all the help you can get, every weapon God has issued, so that when it's all over but the shouting you'll still be on your feet. (Ephesians 6:12–13)

Mighty God, I can't battle this grief alone. Equip me with your weapon, your life-sustaining Word, to battle the discouraging words in my head. Keep me standing, Lord. Don't let me fall.

Day 25 "While the child was alive," he said, "I fasted and wept, thinking God might have mercy on me and the child would live. But now that he's dead, why fast? Can I bring him back now? I can go to him, but he can't come to me." (2 Samuel 12:22–23)

God of eternity, I can't bring my child back. My only hope is your promise that we will see each other again in your presence. Thank you for a reason to cling to you.

Day 26   Meanwhile, right-living people die and no one gives them a thought. God-fearing people are carted off and no one even notices. The right-living people are out of their misery, they're finally at rest. They lived well and with dignity and now they're finally at peace. (Isaiah 57:1–2)

Lord of righteousness, thank you for my child's good life and for taking away his pain. To know he is at peace in your arms is a great comfort. Hold him close until we are together once more in heaven.

Day 27   Are you tired? Worn out? Burned out on religion? Come to me. Get away with me and you'll recover your life. I'll show you how to take a real rest. Walk with me and work with me—watch how I do it. Learn the unforced rhythms of grace. I won't lay anything heavy or ill-fitting on you. Keep company with me and you'll learn to live freely and lightly. (Matthew 11:28–30)

Dear Jesus, I don't need religion to ease the pain of loss. I need you to teach me how to rest. Show me your grace. Walk beside me. Teach me to live in the presence of pain.

Day 28   I look death in the face practically every day I live. Do you think I'd do this if I wasn't convinced of your resurrection and mine as guaranteed by the resurrected Messiah Jesus? (1 Corinthians 15:31)

Dear Jesus, I looked death in the face when you took away my child, and I saw you, the resurrected Lord. Only your victory over death makes the loss bearable. Thank you for being with my child today.

Day 29 He'll wipe every tear from their eyes. Death is gone for good—tears gone, crying gone, pain gone—all the first order of things gone. (Revelation 21:4)

Loving God, I look forward to the day when you will wipe away my tears. I look forward to the day when I will be with my child, in a place where death and tears and pain are gone. Walk with me until that day comes.

Day 30 We know that when Jesus was raised from the dead it was a signal of the end of death-as-the-end. Never again will death have the last word. (Romans 6:9)

Risen Lord, thank you for conquering death. Thank you for showing us that death is not the end. Thank you for the assurance that my child is alive in heaven with you.

Thirty Scriptures to Pray for Your Children

Day 1 Now we look inside, and what we see is that anyone united with the Messiah gets a fresh start, is created new. The old life is gone; a new life burgeons! Look at it! (2 Corinthians 5:17)

Dear life-giving God, you blessed my child with physical life. Now grant him new life in you as he comes to know the Messiah. Unite my child with your Son.

Day 2 Oh yes, you shaped me first inside, then out; you formed me in my mother's womb. I thank you, High God—you're breathtaking! Body and soul, I am marvelously made! I worship in adoration—what a creation! You know me inside and out, you know every bone in my body; you know exactly how I was made, bit by bit, how I was sculpted from nothing into something. (Psalm 139:13–15)

Creator God, you created my child to be the person she is. I praise you for her and ask you to continue your work in her as long as she lives. Draw her to you so she will praise and adore you as her Creator.

Day 3 If I keep my eyes on God, I won't trip over my own feet. (Psalm 25:15)

Dear Lord, teach my child to keep his eyes on you. Guide and direct him as he grows older. Keep him from tripping over his own feet.

Day 4 God isn't late with his promise as some measure lateness. He is restraining himself on account of you, holding back the End because he doesn't want anyone lost. He's giving everyone space and time to change. (2 Peter 3:9)

Dear God who keeps His promises, thank you for restraining your judgment while my child wanders around trying to find you. Give her the space and time she needs to turn her life over to you.

Day 5 The Lord knows the days of the blameless, and their inheritance will be forever. They will not be ashamed in the time of evil, and in the days of famine they will have abundance. (Psalm 37:18–19 NASB)

Righteous God, may my child be blameless before you because she loves your Son. Teach her to trust you in good times and in bad and to find satisfaction in you alone.

Day 6 The person who wins out over the world's ways is simply the one who believes Jesus is the Son of God. (1 John 5:5)

Defender of the weak, be with my child when temptation arises. Strengthen his faith in your Son so he can win the battle against sin.

Day 7 Every desirable and beneficial gift comes out of heaven. The gifts are rivers of light cascading down from the Father of Light. There is nothing deceitful in God, nothing two-faced, nothing fickle. (James 1:17)
Giver of all good gifts, thank you for the wonderful gift of my child and the light she brings to our family. May she grow in grace and come to know you as the one true God who always is who He says He is.

Day 8 For even young people tire and drop out, young folk in their prime stumble and fall. But those who wait upon God get fresh strength. They spread their wings and soar like eagles, they run and don't get tired, they walk and don't lag behind. (Isaiah 40:30–31)
Strong and mighty God, hang on to my child when his faith is weak. Teach him to wait upon you and walk in your strength. Give him endurance for every trial he will face.

Day 9 Before they call out, I'll answer. Before they've finished speaking, I'll have heard. (Isaiah 65:24)
Father who listens, show my child you are listening to her. Answer her before she asks. Finish her sentences for her so she knows that you hear her thoughts.

Day 10 There has never been the slightest doubt in my mind that the God who started this great work in you would keep at it and bring it to a flourishing finish on the very day Christ Jesus appears. (Philippians 1:6)

Dear God, I know you began a great work when you called my child into being. Continue working in his life, conforming him to your will until Christ Jesus comes again.

Day 11 I am the Vine, you are the branches. When you're joined with me and I with you, the relation intimate and organic, the harvest is sure to be abundant. Separated, you can't produce a thing. (John 15:5)
Dear Vinedresser, may my child be a branch on Christ's vine. May she find life in you and stay connected to you forever. May she bear abundant fruit for your kingdom.

Day 12 But God, dear Lord, I only have eyes for you. Since I've run for dear life to you, take good care of me. (Psalm 141:8)
Beautiful Savior, may this verse be the cry of my child's heart. May he have eyes for you alone. May he run to you for life and protection. May he rest in your arms.

Day 13 The disciples shooed them off. But Jesus was irate and let them know it: "Don't push these children away. Don't ever get between them and me. These children are at the very center of life in the kingdom." (Mark 10:14)
Dear Jesus, thank you for loving my child. Don't let anyone get between you and my little one. Keep my child at the very center of your kingdom now and always.

Day 14 Then, gathering the children up in his arms, he laid his hands of blessing on them. (Mark 10:16)
Dear God who hugs His children, gather my child close to you today. Put your hand of blessing on her head. Give her eyes to see your constant, abundant blessings.

Day 15 I look up to the mountains; does my strength come from mountains? No, my strength comes from God, who made heaven, and earth, and mountains. (Psalm 121:1-2)

Dear Refuge and Strength, when my child faces obstacles, focus his eyes on you. Be the one he looks to, the place where he finds his strength.

Day 16 He won't let you stumble, your Guardian God won't fall asleep. Not on your life! Israel's Guardian will never doze or sleep. (Psalm 121:3-4)

Guardian God, keep a constant watch on my child. Don't let her stumble and fall. Protect her when I can't. Be alert to her needs when I can't be there.

Day 17 God's your Guardian, right at your side to protect you—shielding you from sunstroke, sheltering you from moonstroke. (Psalm 121:5-6)

Ever-present and eternal God, stay at my child's side. Be his protection. Be his shield when he faces dangers or sickness. May he sense your presence always.

Day 18 God guards you from every evil, he guards your very life. He guards you when you leave and when you return, he guards you now, he guards you always. (Psalm 121:7-8)

Dear God who guards His children, you have watched over my child since the moment she was conceived. May she learn to trust you with her life in every situation.

Day 19 O dear God, won't you take care of them? We're helpless before this vandal horde ready to attack us. We don't know what to do; we're looking to you. (2 Chronicles 20:12)

Dear God, though I am a parent, I can't protect my child from all evil. When I am helpless, remind me to look to you and trust your wisdom and protection in my child's life.

Day 20 Stories we heard from our fathers, counsel we learned at our mother's knee. We're not keeping this to ourselves, we're passing it along to the next generation—God's fame and fortune, the marvelous things he has done. (Psalm 78:3–4)

Dear Famous One, remind me often to share stories about how you have worked in our family with my children. Prompt me to take advantage of every opportunity to pass faith on to a new generation.

Day 21 Fathers, don't exasperate your children by coming down hard on them. Take them by the hand and lead them in the way of the Master. (Ephesians 6:4)

Lord God, foster a loving relationship between me and my child. Give me wisdom to lead with compassion and give my child a soft heart to follow you, gentle Master.

Day 22 I prayed for this child, and God gave me what I asked for. And now I have dedicated him to God. He's dedicated to God for life. (1 Samuel 1:27–28)

Dear God who answers prayer, thank you for this child. You gave him life, so he is yours. May his whole life be dedicated to honoring you in every way.

Day 23 So eat your meals heartily, not worrying about what others say about you—you're eating to God's glory, after all, not to please them. As a matter of fact, do everything that way, heartily and freely to God's glory. (1 Corinthians 10:31)

Dear Father, work in my child's heart so every facet of her life is a witness of your glory. May she delight in every gift you provide and use them to please you.

Day 24 Pay close attention, friend, to what your father tells you; never forget what you learned at your mother's knee. Wear their counsel like flowers in your hair, like rings on your fingers. (Proverbs 1:8–9)

Dear God of wisdom, may my child hold close everything I have taught him about you. May you be the delight and beauty of his life.

Day 25 But you are my witnesses. . . . You're my handpicked servant so that you'll come to know and trust me, understand both that I am and who I am. Previous to me there was no such thing as a god, nor will there be after me. (Isaiah 43:10)

Master, grant my child a servant's heart toward you. As she serves you, may she come to know and trust in who you are. May she serve you alone.

Day 26 But for you, sunrise! The sun of righteousness will dawn on those who honor my name, healing radiating from its wings. You will be bursting with energy, like colts frisky and frolicking. (Malachi 4:2)

Son of Righteousness, teach my child to honor your name. Heal his heart and give him energy to serve you with the delight and joy of a colt.

Day 27 It's impossible to please God apart from faith. And why? Because anyone who wants to approach God must believe both that he exists and that he cares enough to respond to those who seek him. (Hebrews 11:6)

Dear God, move in my child's heart and bring her to faith so she can approach you. Grant her a life devoted to seeking you, and respond to her needs.

Day 28 But you, O God, are both tender and kind, not easily angered, immense in love, and you never, never quit. (Psalm 86:15)

O God, shower my child with your tenderness and mercy. Be patient with him and guide him to you. Never, never give up on my child. Bring him safely into your kingdom.

Day 29 For the mind set on the flesh is death, but the mind set on the Spirit is life and peace. (Romans 8:6 NASB)

Dear Holy Spirit, move in my child's thoughts so her mind will not be centered on this world but on you. Give her eternal life and peace through Jesus Christ.

Day 30 My son, if sinners entice you, do not consent. (Proverbs 1:10 NASB)

Dear Protector, watch over my child and keep him from temptation. Protect him from selfish people who would take advantage of him. Give him the strength to say no.

Thirty Ways to Pray for Your Child's Character

Day 1   Honesty (Ephesians 4:15)

Day 2   Obedience (1 Peter 2:16–17)

Day 3   Authentic witness (1 Timothy 4:12)

Day 4   Faithfulness (Luke 17:5–6)

Day 5   Maturity (John 15:8)

Day 6   Diligence (Hebrews 12:1)

Day 7   Courage (Deuteronomy 31:6)

Day 8   Servant heart (Philippians 2:3)

Day 9   Generosity (Proverbs 22:9)

Day 10   Responsibility (Galatians 6:4–5)

Day 11   Stewardship (2 Timothy 1:14)

Day 12   Patience (Isaiah 40:31)

Day 13   Compassion (1 John 3:18)

Day 14   Confidence in Christ (Ephesians 2:10)

Day 15   Wisdom (Proverbs 3:6–7)

Day 16   Discernment (1 Samuel 16:7)

Day 17   Joy (Psalm 37:4–5)

Day 18   Peace (John 16:33)

Day 19   Self-control (Titus 2:12)

Day 20   Satisfaction in Christ (John 6:68–69)

Day 21   Knowledge (Jeremiah 33:3)

Day 22   Gentleness (Colossians 3:12)

Day 23   Humility (Titus 3:2)

Day 24   Forgiving (Matthew 6:14–15)

Day 25   A hunger for prayer (Psalm 5:3)

Day 26   Goodness (2 Peter 1:5)

Day 27   Delight in God's Word (Joshua 1:8)

Day 28   Gratitude (Jonah 2:9)

Day 29   Mercy (Zechariah 7:9)

Day 30   Creativity (Colossians 3:10)

God Speaks through His Word

During her son's illness, DeAnn searched her Bible for passages that spoke to her fears, doubts, and grief. At first she wrote them on whatever slips of paper she could find. Later she copied the verses into a journal.

Below are verses God used to speak to her. Some verses may speak to your heart and your circumstances. Some may not. You can trust God to lead you to words of comfort when you seek His voice in His Word.

- When you blame yourself: Psalm 26:2–3; 37:18–19; John 9:1–3
- When it's hard to persevere: Psalm 27:13; Romans 5:2b–5; 8:18; 15:4; James 1:2–4; 1:12; 1 Peter 1:6–7
- When you need a refuge: Psalm 34:4–22; 37:39–40; 46:1

- When you need to guard your speech: James 1:19; 1:26; 1 Peter 3:8–9
- When you need comfort: Psalm 39:7; 2 Corinthians 1:3–4
- When you feel weak: 2 Corinthians 12:10
- When you need to know others have suffered great loss and survived: 2 Samuel 12:22–23; Job 17:10–11
- When you doubt your faith: Job 19:25–27; Psalm 37:3–4; Hebrews 11:1; 1 Peter 4:12–13; 1 John 5:3–5
- When you need confidence: Psalm 19:14; 20:7–8; 1 John 5:14–15
- When you are fearful: Psalm 25:14; 1 John 4:15–18
- When all is dark: Psalm 27:1; 119:105
- When you need a reminder of God's purposes: Psalm 103; 1 Peter 2:9–10
- When you need a quiet heart: Psalm 46:10; 51:10–12; 94:18–19

Appendix C

Lainie's Chart

Use the chart as a template to document types and dosages of medication (meds) and food intake for the day. Customize the times for your schedule. Record vital signs, bowel movements, and other important information. The miscellaneous space can be used to communicate to those people caring for your child.

Date _____

Time	O2	HR	RR	FiO2	Miscellaneous
12 midnight					
5 am					
9 am					
12 noon					
1:30 pm					
4 pm					
6 pm					
Meds and time	**Dose**				
(Name of med)					
6 am					
2 pm					
10 pm					
(Name of med)					
7 am					
7 pm					
(Name of med)					
5 am					
6 pm					
(Name of med)					
1 pm					

O2—oxygen reading
HR—heart rate
RR—respiratory rate
FiO2—amount of oxygen given

Appendix D

Nancy's In-Home Nursing Care Interview Questions

If you need nursing care or are unhappy with your child's present quality of care, Nancy's questions may be helpful when interviewing home health care or respite agencies.

1. How do you train your nurses or verify that they have training? What continuing training do you require? (Ask specifically about your child's situation: trach, g-tube, oxygen, Diastat, injections, etc.)

2. How do you orient a nurse to a patient? Is a home visit required? How long is it? How many visits? Will I be notified before someone comes over?

3. How do you a handle a nurse being late? Will the agency inform me of a nurse's tardiness or will the nurse contact me directly? How will I be notified if a different nurse is coming in place of the scheduled one?

4. How do you handle a nurse who does something unacceptable like falling asleep? Will you send that nurse again?

5. What communication style do you use? How often do schedulers or case managers call, e-mail, or visit the house? How am I to communicate problems? How soon will problems with nurses or schedules be corrected?

6. How many nurses do you have in the area? Will you need to recruit some to cover the case? Is the agency willing to pay nurses overtime until the case is fully staffed?

7. What materials does the agency supply for the nurses? How often are the materials delivered to my home and how do they arrive? What if the nurse runs out of supplies?

8. Does the agency monitor daily therapies and cleanings the same way it monitors medicines? If not, what kind of monitoring system is used for daily therapies and cleanings?

9. How often is a nursing staff schedule created: monthly, biweekly, or weekly? Does the agency create all the branch schedules at the same time, like at the beginning of the month? When do you need schedule requests for the next planning period? When can I expect to receive the schedule? How many cases does each scheduler handle?

10. How are hours from missed shifts handled? Are they lost if a replacement can't be found for that day, or can they be used for a double shift later? Is the answer the same for private insurance and GAPP/Medicaid programs?

11. Can the nurse accompany me to doctor visits? If not, what must be done to request it? What are the guidelines for the nurse to accompany me on other nonmedical trips from the house?

Of course, you may have other questions pertaining to your child's specific conditions, and questions or issues may arise as you work with an agency. Be sure to write down the answers each agency gives to your questions and keep them. Also, keep e-mail correspondence with an agency in case an answer changes at a later date.

Index

accessibility, 167, 170, 171

accommodations and adaptations, 159, 227–28, 262–64, 267

adoption, 238, 248–250

adult children: coping skills, 238, 240, 244–45; estate and financial planning, 254–56; living arrangements, 163, 238–39, 263; special needs trust, 255–59

advocacy: child self-advocacy, 161; at church, 170–71, 262–64; in community, 168–70; at diagnosis,19–20, 38–39; effectiveness of, 25–28; with government agencies, 149–51; in the hospital, 62–64, 66, 74–76; with insurance companies, 38–40; mental health treatment and, 246–48; through prayer, 51–53, 224–25; research, 20–21, 28–31; residential placement and, 151–54; at school, 26, 157–58, 160–62

anxiety, 102, 106, 248, 249, 264

assistance: educational, 159–61; financial, 43; government,147–52, 254–55; lodging, 41; meals, 41, 43, 128; philanthropic, 44; private and non-profit, 150–51; travel, 43; volunteer, 128–29, 136–37

attitude, 27–28, 66, 235–40

Bible: characters, 221–26; online versions and helps, 93; reading plans, 94; study, 92–94

hospital personnel: care team, 66,
70–76, 159, 190–91, 193–94,
201, 211; chaplain, 41, 64, 93,
108, 116, 201, 213; child life
specialist, 21–22, 32, 73, 75, 80,
81, 114, 116, 247–48; nurses, 32,
40, 71–73, 75, 81; patient representative, 74–76; phlebotomists,
73; physicians, 39, 70–72; social
worker, 32, 39–43, 64, 73, 75,
86–87, 107–8, 116, 126, 129,
149, 152, 247; therapists, 72–73

independent living, 163, 240, 254

insurance, 28, 38–40, 42–43, 126,
147, 255–58

job. *See* employment

legal documents, 257–58

loss. *See* grief

marriage, 86–87, 101–5, 106–8,
211–12

Medicaid, 147, 150–51, 255

medical waiver programs, 150, 255

medically needy programs, 151

Medicare, 150

memory-making, 114–15, 192–94,
204

mental illness, 106, 243–49

military families, 126

notebook. *See* care notebook

nurses, 32, 40, 71–73, 75, 81

occupational therapy, 72

organization, 21, 27, 31–32, 128–29,
160–62

pain and palliative care, 74, 190–91,
200–201

patient and family-centered care,
32, 62, 64, 66, 70, 72

physical therapy, 72

physicians: advice from 149, 238,
244; communication with,
21–22, 26–27, 75; hospital stay
and, 63, 65, 70–72, 84–85;
scheduling and, 125

play therapy, 248

post-traumatic stress disorder
(PTSD), 106, 112, 243–50, 262

prayer: character development and,
33, 91–92; for children, 224–25,
261–62, 264–66; dependence
upon God through, 54, 66,
90–91; determining priorities
and, 134–35; at diagnosis,
21–22, 44; fruits of the Spirit
and, 265; God's sovereignty
and, 51–53, 90–91, 93; grief
and, 221–26; guilt and, 105,
177–78; importance of, 51–53;
Jesus and, 52; journal, 93, 268;
priorities, 134–35; questions
about, 51–53; recognizing
opportunities for, 137–138;
reflection and, 181–82; using
Scripture in, 51–53, 181–82

preschool, 25, 81, 147, 169–70, 249

priorities, 33, 134–41

relationships with: children, 114–18,
139–41, 193–95, 211, 266–68;
extended family, 107–8, 118–19;
God, 66, 109, 137–39, 141,
226; hospital personnel, 74–75;
school personnel, 161; spouse,
103, 106–9, 211–12

research, 20–21, 28–31

respiratory therapy, 72, 139

roles and routines, 135–36, 211, 236

Scripture: about death of children,
221–25; grief and, 226; guilt

Note to the Reader

The publisher invites you to share your response to the message of this book by writing Discovery House Publishers, P.O. Box 3566, Grand Rapids, MI 49501, U.S.A. For information about other Discovery House books, music, videos, or DVDs, contact us at the same address or call 1-800-653-8333. Find us on the Internet at http://www.dhp.org/ or send e-mail to books@dhp.org.

What readers are saying about
A Different Dream for My Child: Meditations for Parents of Critically or Chronically Ill Children . . .

"The trauma and drama of a sick child is a journey of its own kind. Gratefully Jolene has tenderly come to the heart-aid of these families. If you have experienced or are living in deep sorrow brought on by your child's condition, I recommend that you open this book and allow the balm of understanding to meet you where you are at . . . to help ease your ongoing ache, your loneliness, and your feelings of isolation."

Patsy Clairmont
Author of *Catching Fireflies* and Women of Faith speaker

"No words can change the diagnosis, but there are those who can help parents change their attitude. Jolene Philo understands those cries because of the experience with her son, Allen. I highly recommend this book from a mother who opens her heart on every page."

Cecil Murphey
New York Times best-selling author of more than 100 books,
including *When Someone You Love Has Cancer*

"What a tremendously helpful and inspiring book! Having two chronically ill children myself, I was amazed at how well acquainted Philo was with the private pain, grief, guilt, and loneliness I have experienced trying to cope with it all. With each devotion, my spirit was lifted into a hope I have rarely felt in the midst of the battle. I highly recommend this book to any parent whose dreams for their children have been sidetracked by illness."

Rene Gutteridge
Author of *Never the Bride* and *My Life as a Doormat*

"The examples of comfort and shared experience will benefit all who read this book. Chronic sorrow follows chronic disease, and the reflections offered are excellent in addressing this. Every problem discussed is 'right on' and pulls out personal recollections of many of my patients. I would recommend it to families and caretakers alike."

David H. Van Dyke, MD
Pediatric neurologist

"A Different Dream for My Child offers the right words for those painful moments when everything seems wrong. The author's personal stories create common ground with readers; her prayers express what grieving parents feel but can't always articulate; her reflective postscripts nudge readers to move past the 'now' and onto the 'what's next?' Philo's book is like a gentle balm prescribed for persons bruised and battered by circumstances."

Holly G. Miller
Editor, *The Saturday Evening Post*

"Powerful, insightful, and candidly honest, Jolene Philo's book *A Different Dream for My Child* is a treasured companion for those who've journeyed the heart-bending path of caring for a chronically or critically ill child. Written with insight, passion, and wisdom, Jolene's words deliver both comfort and biblical counsel on the diverse and complex emotional, spiritual, relational, and practical aspects of caring for sick children. This book is a celebration of hope in the God of comfort who walks beside us in the midst of our pain."

Shelly Beach
Award-winning author of
Precious Lord, Take My Hand and *Ambushed by Grace*